Selling

For Entrepreneurs

Selling

For Entrepreneurs

Kathryn Lennon

PEARSON
Prentice Hall
BUSINESS

Harlow, England • London • New York • Boston • San Francisco • Toronto • Sydney • Singapore • Hong Kong
Tokyo • Seoul • Taipei • New Delhi • Cape Town • Madrid • Mexico City • Amsterdam • Munich • Paris • Milan

PEARSON EDUCATION LIMITED

Edinburgh Gate
Harlow CM20 2JE
Tel: +44 (0)1279 623623
Fax: +44 (0)1279 431059
Website: www.pearsoned.co.uk

First published in Great Britain in 2009

ISBN: 978-0-273-72492-6

British Library Cataloguing-in-Publication Data
A catalogue record for this book is available from the British Library

Library of Congress Cataloging-in-Publication Data
Lennon, Kathryn.
  Selling for entrepreneurs / Kathryn Lennon. -- 1st ed.
    p. cm.
  Includes index.
  ISBN 978-0-273-72492-6 (pbk.)
  1. Selling--Psychological aspects. I. Title.
  HF5438.25.L46 2009
  658.85--dc22
                          2009017901

10 9 8 7 6 5 4 3 2 1
13 12 11 10 09

Series text design by Design Deluxe
All cartoons © Jurgen Wolff
Typeset in 9/13pt, Swis721 Lt BT by 30
Printed and bound in Great Britain by Henry Ling Ltd, Dorchester, Dorset

The publisher's policy is to use paper manufactured from sustainable forests.

Praise

'I always say that in the modern business, everybody sells. This how-to guide will take you through every stage in the process.'

MIKE SOUTHON, *FINANCIAL TIMES* COLUMNIST,
BESTSELLING AUTHOR AND ENTREPRENEUR MENTOR

'Romancing your customer means building a lasting relationship, and Kathryn's approach to sales gives you the strongest possible platform to do this. This entrepreneurial approach to selling is exactly what businesses should be delivering, day in and day out. This woman knows her stuff!'

ANGI EGAN, AUTHOR AND MANAGING DIRECTOR, PURE VISION UK LTD

Contents

Part One The foundations of selling

Part Two The sales process

Part three The secrets of selling

...for Entrepreneurs

Being an entrepreneur can be the path to controlling your own life and to financial success. With the *For Entrepreneurs* series, it doesn't have to be a lonely journey any more. Our expert authors guide you through all phases of starting and running a business, with practical advice every step of the way. Whether you are just getting started or want to grow your business, whether you want to become a skilled marketer or salesperson or just want to get your business finances under control, there is a *For Entrepreneurs* book ready to be your experienced, friendly and supportive business coach. Our titles include:

→ *How to Start Your Own Business for Entrepreneurs*

→ *How to Grow Your Business for Entrepreneurs*

→ *Selling for Entrepreneurs*

→ *Marketing for Entrepreneurs*

→ *Book-keeping and Accounts for Entrepreneurs*

You'll find more information and more support on our website: **www.forentrepreneursbooks.com**.

Jurgen Wolff, General Editor

About the author

Following a successful career as a marketing and organisational psychology specialist and consultant working around the world with blue chip companies and household names, **Kathryn Lennon** founded Tangerine Trees Business Consultancy, specialising in innovative no-nonsense advice utilising the latest technologies, and shattering the myths that consultancy must be expensive or shrouded in mystery.

Kathryn is a radio broadcaster, speaker, consultant, trainer and writer, getting information to business owners in the way they want it, as well as running her own successful small business.

Kathryn is a Prince's Trust mentor and a patron of the Big Issue Foundation, as well as a contender for the Guinness World Record for the World's Largest Business Consultancy.

She lives in the West Midlands with her fiancé.

Acknowledgements

Firstly I'd like to thank Robert Ashton, Pearson's champion racehorse, for his support and encouragement in converting my thoughts and ideas into the visible written words you hold in your hand, and for introducing me to Caroline Jordan, Editorial Assistant extraordinaire at Pearson.

I'm indebted to Jurgen Wolff for his expertise in editing this *For Entrepreneurs* series and for his vision of the brave new world we aimed to create. Of course, my gratitude also extends to the many giants whose shoulders I climbed upon momentarily in an attempt to tie their genius into this theme of twenty-first century selling.

And I am forever grateful to the family and friends who supported me, and to my fiancé for the constant supply of cups of tea and hugs required to transform ideas into coherent text.

But I'd also like to acknowledge the people who may never even know that this book has been created – Steve Wright, trainer with the Sandler Sales Institute, for his unending motivation, difficult questions and general belief that there had to be a better way to sell. Mike Southon, co-author of the *Beermat Entrepreneur*, whose books have provided advice and solace in the early days of starting a business. And Anita Roddick, late great founder of The Body Shop, and my hero in business and ethics.

And, last but by no means least, to the prospects who have worn me down, dented my confidence and honed my sales skills in ways I never could have anticipated when I started out in business. Those experiences proved to me that it must be possible to get fabulous sales and still be a nice person.

To all our business successes,

Kathryn Lennon

Introduction

If the word 'sales' makes you a little nervous – maybe because of bad experiences you've had yourself with salespeople or because you think you need to be a massive extrovert in order to sell – relax, I am about to show you a different way.

Whilst I've run my own business for a number of years, and taken a passionate interest in sales, I've never been an advocate of the kind of hard-nosed approach that has given even the word 'sales' a negative connotation for many people.

The approach I was first taught, and indeed the one I often experienced, seemed to be the 'wear them down until they give in' strategy. Whenever I tried this myself in business, I felt uncomfortable, rude and even apologetic. That's why I was delighted when I began to uncover glimmers of *real* selling. The kind that makes you feel glad you got into a conversation in the first place.

When I began using that approach myself, I could literally see harassed prospects take a sigh of relief, knowing that if the conversation wasn't revealing any real wins for them, they had my clear permission, in fact my insistence, that they should say so.

By ditching the outdated sales thinking and getting twenty-first century selling techniques, I promise you'll be a step closer to fabulous sales results and, probably just as importantly, you'll still be a nice person.

Selling is a journey, and depending on the line of business you're in, a sale can be quite a ride. I've separated out the chapters that follow to give you details on every aspect of the sales process, from planning to presentation to closing, so you can plan for the twists and turns ahead of you.

Equally importantly, though, is the mindset that goes with those tactics. More and more tactics do not make a better salesperson. Your self-image, your confidence, your focus and your understanding of the journey that your buyer is taking will set you apart from the masses. Combining those powerful tools with your personality and sense of humour will make selling an enjoyable experience for buyer and seller.

I really hope you enjoy what follows. And I really, really hope that you start applying it. Knowledge is only potential power, and attitude is led by behaviour.

The foundations of selling

Part One

How and why people buy

Chapter One

You must understand how and why people buy.

This is the part that all traditional sales books skip. They tend to move straight into tactics and mindsets for you as the seller to adopt. But today's entrepreneur knows that all the powerful tactics in the world won't convince someone who's not ready to buy.

In this chapter we will look at the complexities of your buyer's mind, understand the buying process and look at buyer personality types. Then we will map these pieces of information on to your selling process. And finally we will discuss the potential damage of conflicting messages in your sales.

As I am prone to repeating to my own clients, some would say like a broken record, you can't know enough about why people buy from you. Because, as you start to understand why they buy, you are in a position to influence them to take action.

In order to sell effectively, here are some of the things you must understand about your target audience:

→ With what do they associate pain?

→ With what do they associate pleasure?

→ What self-image do they want to attain or maintain?

→ Who buys you, who uses you?

You must also understand how your product impacts their lives:

→ Do they consider your offering a business case, a life essential or an impulse purchase?

→ Will it increase their revenue, their free time, their sex appeal?

→ Will it help them with legal compliance?

→ Will it save them time or money, or reduce business overheads?

→ Will it make their children happy, make their partner fancy them, make their neighbours jealous?

And even if you sell to businesses, commercial and personal needs are both factors in business-to-business buying decisions.

The four secrets of how people buy

People like buying. Oh yes, we do. What we don't like is the feeling of being pressured or forced to buy. But if something is genuinely going to make our life better, easier, happier or richer, don't we want to know about it? Cynicism is an inevitability in today's world of mass information; the world of gullible audiences for travelling medicine men is long gone. What we like is to be sold to well, and that includes pointing out the best solution for our needs and managing our expectations of that solution to avoid 'buyer's remorse' or cognitive dissonance.

In other words

Cognitive dissonance is anxiety that results from simultaneously holding contradictory or otherwise incompatible attitudes, beliefs or the like, as when one likes a person but disapproves strongly of one of their habits.

Good selling makes us feel comfortable and in control, respects our time and our money, answers our questions and gives us options. Friendly human interactions actually release endorphins (hormones that create feelings of pleasure), because we are ultimately social creatures and we gain enjoyment from the connection. People buy people. Even when we buy a brand we make associations to personalise it, and good branding reinforces those human characteristics. All these buying decisions are emotional. When we give something a logical reason, it is because we have invested more emotion in that reason than in any other option.

There are four fundamentals of buyer behaviour that the entrepreneurial seller keeps as their mantra:

→ People buy people.
→ People buy what they want.
→ The fear of loss is more powerful than the pleasure of gain.
→ We buy the things that best match the benefits we seek.

The buying process

During this buying process we pass through clear stages, known historically as 'AIDA', or Attentive, Interested, Desirous and Active, which are discussed in much more detail in Chapter Ten. Two more recent additions to that buying process are Contemplative, where we are vaguely aware of a new product or behaviour, but it hasn't yet grabbed our attention, and Maintaining, where we have made a purchase and taken action, and now we look to keep up the lifestyle, benefit realisation or good feeling that we got from making our purchase.

This process is often represented by a funnel. A funnel shows the process that each and every one of our buyers goes through, and is therefore the process we must match as entrepreneurial sellers.

Depending on the product or service your business sells and the industry sectors you operate in, working through the funnel stages could involve anything from a 15-minute conversation to a 12-month contract negotiation.

The types of customers

We humans are social creatures and our behaviour is consistent with our view of ourselves, our environment and the expectations of our peers and relatives. Most of what we do, we do because of other people. And these psychological variables, these components that make us the individuals we are, include our perception of the world that gives us our emotional response to certain brands or messages, our motivation for doing whatever we do, our approach to learning and solving problems, our memory and our attitude to life.

There are obviously infinite combinations of those components, but don't glaze over just yet! Helpfully, the relevance to us as sellers is that the potential variations actually sum up as several buyer personality types, no doubt some more relevant than others to your particular industry, as the following table demonstrates:

BUYER PERSONALITY TYPES

Type	Characteristics	Handling them
The apathetic type	Often negative or disinterested, they may seem like they're never going to buy anything.	They sometimes surprise you! Don't respond with excessive positive messages.
Task-focused buyers	Want results, deliverables and outcomes.	Bore them with features at your peril.
Self-actualising buyers	They know exactly what they want and have a pretty clear idea of what they'll pay.	If you offer it, they'll take it. Make sure they know you offer it.
Analytical types	Want all the details clear in their minds.	Make sure you've got facts to hand.
The emotional prospect	These can be particularly difficult to spot early in the conversation, as their concern is for the views and responses of others.	Ask good questions and you'll soon be able to determine this buyer's reliance on the views of others, including you.

You've probably read a dozen times that it's vital to discover the buyer's motives, check any assumptions you could be making and link your offer to benefits for the buyer. But do you know why?

Our potential buyers work through a series of stages in the buying process, the AIDA stages, and nothing you can do can speed that up or make them skip stages. But you can help them move smoothly from one stage to the next, you can understand the ones that get lost along the way and check that you are catering for all personality types, and you can focus extensively on not getting in your own way with roadblocks like conflicting messages, shoddy products or poor service.

Getting past customer roadblocks

Why are these roadblocks so important? Have you ever just had 'a hunch' that something wasn't right for you – a product, a company, a salesperson? Well, our minds can only hold seven pieces of current information. If something jars with that information, or contradicts it, we might not even know why – we just feel that it's 'wrong'.

This 'magical number seven' was first discussed by the eminent psychologist George A. Miller. His research proved that seven is the number of items or chunks that we can hold in our short-term memory. So while most people can generally hold around seven numbers in mind for a short period, almost everyone finds it difficult to hold ten digits in mind.

For your business, the span of these chunks could be promotional advertising, your brand, the products, your store, any celebrity endorsement and other people wearing/using the product. They could also be the experiential difference between the quality of service you claim in writing and the actual delivery.

And when we take on the buying and selling roles, the power of seven applies to both parties. It's the limit of what we can know and experience in a short time, and when it's done right it moves us through the AIDA funnel towards an action, a sale.

Constantly chasing prospects after they've shown an interest can be soul-destroying and border on pushy salesmanship, something the entrepreneur would never dream of! But by having a longer sales process, prospects are moved from one stage to the next over a period of time, are constantly informed and educated, and are reminded of your services. And as this is designed to be professional and courteous, customers never feel intimidated or pushed.

Using the stages

Most businesses have only two or three planned stages in their sales process. They might follow up a website enquiry with a phone call and an email. Or they might send follow-up letters or arrange an appointment after someone requests a brochure. But more often than not, a customer picks up a price list or attends an event, and we're too apprehensive about being pushy to follow it up.

For instance, business communications to a very broad audience with varying requirements would usually take the form of public relations (PR), websites and advertising. As you can't anticipate the people that will see these messages, you must be absolutely clear about how they can move to the next stage if this is of interest to them. And the next piece of communication they receive should reinforce their initial interest and build on it.

For example, your advertising might offer an invitation to a relevant exhibition where prospective customers can learn even more about your offering. Your website could provide downloads of information that are useful to your target audience. Your PR could refer to specific networking events and seminars that your company hosts.

Each of these communications will include specific calls to action where the prospect receives more information, reinforcing their interest and creating desire.

What does this mean to you? Well, it means the difference between applying a selection of the excellent sales theories that exist in the world to an audience who pay little, or inconsistent, attention and applying the right theory to the right prospect at the right time.

Where in your prospect's life does your product or service fit?

Let's take a closer look at how customer motivation gives you the key to how to sell to them:

Buyer motivation	Which means...	Business examples
Pain now	Avoiding or getting out of something immediately	Doctors, dentists, petrol stations, weight-loss groups
Pleasure now	Gaining from something immediately	Hairdressers, beauty salons, fast food restaurants
Pain in the future	Avoiding or getting out of something potential	Insurers, accountants, gyms, DIY
Pleasure in the future	Gaining from something potential	Travel agents, investments, dating agencies
Interest	Knowing a bit more about something	Prospect collects brochures from all types of business

Naturally, one of the things buyers think about is the cost of whatever you are offering. Cost is not just money, it's absolute cost. Could buying your product or service increase your customer's maintenance, insurance or legal bills? Could using your offer mean stopping something they currently do and enjoy? For instance, a weight-loss subscription service is likely to stop their regular consumption of fast food and other enjoyable junk. Could it change the view their peers or social group has of them? If so, your selling process has to reassure the buyers that what they will gain is greater than what they will lose.

With these potential outcomes in your audience's head, being seen as an expert in your field helps to soothe the fevered brow of a prospect fearing the next step. And if you operate in a crowded marketplace, this has got to be good news. You are the one they seek when questions need answering.

The ideal sales process should contain no less than seven stages, although the more the better. You should set your sights on ten. And each component of each stage should highlight your knowledge and expertise to help your prospect understand the answers to their questions. These sales stages can (and should) include the following sales tools:

- → advertising and PR (press relations, i.e. the media);
- → direct communications – email, letters, invitations, etc.;
- → your website, web downloads or reports;
- → phone and email conversations;
- → face-to-face conversations;
- → newsletters and magazines;
- → special occasion cards;
- → seminars, exhibitions and events;
- → brochures and literature;
- → consultations and demonstrations.

The following example illustrates the AIDA stages a customer passes through during a typical buying process.

Stage 1: Attentive

How do you decide you want to buy a particular product or service? It could be that your DVD player stops working and you now have to look for a new one, or you're stressed and need a holiday or in pain and need a dentist. So you have a problem or a new need. Let's use the holiday example. At this stage we would be looking for sales information that is general – advertisements and websites from stores offering travel and holidays would be obvious tools.

Stage 2: Interested

So we have a need – we want a holiday. But where should we go to address our particular buyer motivation of achieving pleasure in the future by reducing our stress? Customers often use social proof to help them through their purchase decision. Sources of proof could be family, friends and neighbours who may have made the same decision you have in mind. Alternatively they may ask the salespeople or other customers, or read specialist magazines such as *Traveller*, to help with their purchase decision. This is known as the product/supplier choice stage – we know what we want to buy in general terms. Sales tools at this stage that help answer our questions could include magazine and online reviews, face-to-face conversations with salespeople and resort advertisements.

Social proof, also known as **informational social influence**, is a psychological phenomenon that occurs in ambiguous social situations where people are unable to determine the appropriate mode of behaviour. Assuming that surrounding people possess more knowledge about the situation, they will copy their behaviour.

Stage 3: Desirous

We know we really want a holiday. And specifically we want a holiday to reduce our stress. Will that be achieved through sunshine, pampering, low expenditure, sightseeing or interaction with others? Customers allocate 'attribute factors' to certain products, almost like a point scoring system, which they work out in their mind regarding which option to purchase. This means that customers know what features from you and your rivals will benefit them and they attach different degrees of importance to each attribute.

For example, sunbathing may be better at Resort A and sightseeing at Resort B, but new experiences are more important to you than a tan. And Resort C offers a combination of both sights and sunshine but costs more. How important is finance in the decision? Customers usually have some sort of brand preference with companies, as they or their friends may have had a good history with one in particular. For obvious reasons, this is called the brand choice stage – are you one of the options in your prospect's mind when they reach this stage? Sales tools here could include relationship building events, DVDs and testimonials.

Stage 4: Active

Through the evaluation process discussed above, consumers will reach their final purchase decision, and for some consumers the act of purchasing can be just as rewarding as the thing they buy. Purchase of our holiday could be through the store, the web or over the phone. During this stage, we make our supplier choice, purchase timing and purchase amount decisions. But we don't do this alone. Even if we are

Selling for Entrepreneurs

buying a holiday from an internet store because it offers the best value, interest and desire can still be created for other products, related or not to our original purchase, which can affect our purchase timing and amount. An expert seller could note our interest in sightseeing and suggest a guidebook or a nearby location. Other sales tools at this point could highlight partnership deals with other related businesses, as well as specific offers and guarantees.

So our very simplistic example shows us deciding we need a holiday, identifying the specific need of a stress-reducing holiday, choosing a destination and making a purchase with a supplier.

Sales pitfalls to avoid

In our seller role, we could actually have lost the sale by making any one of a number of fatal mistakes, such as:

→ Inconsistency in our intended and unintended sales messages, such as our website or advertising, causing one of the seven information chunks within our audience's mind to be taken up with conflicting information.

→ Ongoing brand development or long-term changes and improvements could lead to differing presentation of our brand and products, but our customer wasn't involved in all those meetings and discussions and is only seeing the information at that moment – don't confuse them!

→ Lack of coordination in all sales activity could be perceived by our target audiences as being a lack of coordination within our business.

→ Failure to appreciate the type of customer we are selling to is guaranteed to give one big, screaming message – 'we don't know our customers'.

→ Trying to give non-technical people too much information could be confusing. Is our audience likely to be elderly and in need of bigger print or easier access to our premises? Does our service fit their needs?

→ It's almost impossible to influence someone else's thoughts and actions with one sales tool. We need to become experts in our fields, and we do that by answering questions and helping them to the next stage of the process.

→ Communicating more than one message at a time is almost certain to confuse the recipient. It might make perfect sense to us, but remember that we work in our business all day, every day. And the more internal meetings and conversations that have led to the creation of an external message, the more need there is to ensure that we're not making assumptions about the current state of our audience's mind.

→ The objective of every sales activity is to move our prospect on to the next stage in the funnel. If the objectives of your activity aren't completely clear, prospects will lack decisiveness.

Be prepared

Not every prospect will reach you at the very beginning of your sales process. In our example above, we had already decided we wanted a holiday, weighed up our options and done some research before we committed to the seller. By making sure you have your sales activity planned in every section of the funnel, a customer who comes to you at any stage in their buying process can get the information they need and fall seamlessly into your selling process. Also remember that a prospect may want to step sideways and get more information within each of the stages, so a prospect who responds to your advertising might want to attend an event, request a brochure and be added to your email list before they're ready to move forward.

If a prospect was standing at your shop counter deciding how to pay when they place their order, you wouldn't start showing them your advertising instead, as the desire is already there and they are ready to take action. Equally, if someone had just read a piece of your PR, it might be too early to send them all your testimonials and guarantees as they have not necessarily recognised a need for your products or services.

The sales armoury in your funnel will vary for businesses across

'The Adult learner' Malcolm knowles
9781856178112.   £29.99.

'reflective practice' gillie bowlan . 9781848602120

W

Waterstones   £23.99.

11-17 Castle Street, Norwich, Norfolk, NR2 1PB   T. 0843 290 8519   F. 0843 290 8520   E. manager@norwich-castlestreet.waterstones.com
Registered as Waterstones Booksellers Limited. Registered in England No 610095.
Waterstones.com

different industries, but try to think bigger than simply focusing on what your competitors do or how your company works. Think about how customers buy, and how they compare their buying experiences with every other company they shop with, not just your competitors.

Who is your target customer?

Tony Robbins, the American motivational speaker, identified six human needs that are in direct competition with each other and cause constant change in our lives. Naturally these have an effect on what we buy, from whom and when. Let's look at these six needs:

OUR CONFLICTING HUMAN NEEDS

Certainty. Of course there is no absolute certainty, but we want to be certain the car will start, the water will flow from the tap when we turn it on and the currency we use will hold its value.	*Variety*. At the same time we want certainty, we also crave variety. Paradoxically, there needs to be enough uncertainty to provide spice and adventure in our lives.
Significance. Deep down, we all want to be important. We want our life to have meaning and significance.	*Connection/love*. It would be hard to argue against the need for love. We want to feel part of a community. We want to be cared for and cared about.
Growth. To become better, to improve our skills, to stretch ourselves and excel at things may be more evident in some than others, but it's there.	*Contribution*. The desire to contribute something of value, to help others, to make the world a better place than we found it is in all of us.

Deciding who you should sell to is one of the most important business decisions you will ever make. Market segmentation is all about communicating with groups of people who have similar needs and think in similar ways. But the above grid reminds the entrepreneurial seller that prospects are also human beings with complex needs and perceptions.

In the twenty-first century, we are all inundated by sales messages. It is said that we are swamped by some 3,000 sales messages on an average day. So how do you ensure that your sales messages get through?

When you talk to a defined group (a market segment) about their specific concerns, it is much easier to get their attention. After all, you are talking about their challenges and their issues. You are seen as an expert. People like dealing with specialists.

So, the first step is to sort your sales process out, so that it delivers consistent messages to your target market segments. We'll talk about this much more as we go along. If you adopt this approach your business will be much more focused. This means that your audience will be more prepared to listen to you. In addition, as your messages are not being scattered they are more likely to be repeated to the right people. This, in turn, helps with brand recognition. This is how 'famous-name brands' and successful businesses are built.

Effective selling ensures there is integration and consistency in all of your sales and marketing. Very often, the focus for this starts and ends with your intended communications. That means your designed, created or printed communications, like brochures, signage, website, case studies, PR and advertising.

But if something isn't perceived by the other person, it doesn't exist. So if your expensive, high-quality brochure is sitting on top of your tatty shop counter, any messages you try to communicate about quality and exclusivity simply won't be perceived that way.

The power of consistency

If *all* your sales messages are consistent, your audience doesn't have to reassess the information and try to find the common themes. Instead, it can concentrate on the seven chunks of information that you are intentionally communicating. So you should be looking to ensure that you are consistent in all the following areas of your business.

Yourself

Be true to what you believe and what your business represents. Your own brand values, the quality and service you commit to and the things that you're passionate about.

Your actions

It is important that you behave in line with the messages your company promotes. Customer service is vital to your business. Do you state great service? Is that the impression that your customer perceives?

Your face-to-face communications

Do you and your teams speak the same words that you write? Inconsistency here is usually one of the clear signs that a company has 'outsourced' its sales and marketing, either to an external supplier or, more often, to an internal member of staff who is tasked with creating perceptions on behalf of the whole business.

Your company signals

If you are claiming quality or exclusivity or technological superiority, how are you displaying that? You may have made great investments into the manufacturing, technology or distribution arms of your business, but if your customer doesn't see that, it won't be the message they receive. You could start by ensuring that you find ways to demonstrate these areas of investment, in relation to the needs it meets for them. And also be aware of the signals that ageing posters, cheap furniture and tatty carpets, or directors' parking spaces right outside the door, give to visiting customers.

Your products and services

After you've created consistency in all your effective, integrated business activity and your unintended communications, do your products and services ruin all your hard work? Although your offering itself might be all the things you've claimed (and it should be), it could undo all your hard work if it arrives in poor or scruffy packaging, or is delivered as an anticlimax to the buying process, perhaps late or with mistakes.

Your after-sales communications

So your customer has come with you through the buying process. They bought your product or service based on all the needs it would meet for them, and they're keen to start using it. But they can't quite get it to work, it's missing a vital piece or they just want to ask your advice. And now they have to call a premium rate number and wait in a queue. And when they get through, no one can trace their details or help with their query. This is nightmare scenario of unintended communications, and one we've probably all experienced.

Comments about you by other organisations

Although you can't hope to control what others feel or say about you, make sure your intended and unintended communications don't exclude those groups who don't and won't buy from you. Their views and opinions could still influence customers who do buy from you.

Five focus questions

Here are five questions to help you focus on how and why people buy from you.

What do you want your sales message to say?

What is the value in what you're saying and what are the consequences? Start by clarifying what your objectives are. Where in the sales funnel is this particular sales message? What do you want your prospect to do when they receive your messages? A successful sales message will answer questions and lead the prospect forward.

Decide what you want to say about your business or product/service. This is harder than it sounds. How does your product meet their needs?

Who do you want to say it to?

What segment of people are you trying to reach with your sales message? What do they currently think about you? What do you want them to think about you? What human needs does your product magnify or negate?

How do you want to present your message?

Is it a face-to-face message, a piece of written sales literature or an interactive experience? Focus on the main benefits that your product offers customers and present them in the clearest way. Try not to use too much jargon, and if you do have to use it, then explain what it means in simple terms. And make sure any potentially conflicting messages or information are removed.

How do you want to distribute your message?

What route is best for your customer? Is your message complex, immediate, transient? Although using the telephone to book appointments is rightly given pride of place in many a sales book, and you can learn much more about the best ways to succeed at it in Chapter Four, is it actually the best technique for your customers? There are many other ways that your sales message could and should be distributed.

When should you send your message?

Are there certain times of the day that your customers prefer to receive sales calls or make appointments? Are there days of the week when your counter sales excel? Does your product have a seasonality, like end-of-year accounts production, gym membership or ice-cream? And how far in advance of delivery do your customers need to make a decision about purchase?

> **People will forget what you said. They will forget what you did. But they will never forget how you made them feel.** MAYA ANGELOU

Web bonus

At our website, **www.forentrepreneursbooks.com**, click on the 'Selling for Entrepreneurs' button. On the link for Chapter One you'll find your own downloadable sales funnel that you can populate with your current sales activities and look for areas to add more.

Key points

→ As buyers, we pass through a process traditionally known as AIDA. We take actions (or not) based on how we feel at each stage.

→ Buyers' view of themselves, their world and the things that they aspire to have and achieve will influence their purchasing decisions.

→ We only remember seven things at a time, and when those things contradict each other we feel uncomfortable in proceeding.

→ But seven (or more) consistent sales messages could help us through the AIDA process towards a sale.

→ As sellers, we can increase our chances of saying the right things to the right audiences by creating segments.

Next steps

What action will you take to apply the information in this chapter? By when will you do it?

_____

_____

_____

_____

The psychology of selling

Chapter Two

No successful entrepreneur ever acts without a clear understanding of themselves and their own role, or a fundamental understanding of their business and their products, before they start trying to sell.

In this chapter we will look at the importance of knowing yourself. The chapter will build into an understanding of personal development and the barriers to this, namely limiting self-beliefs and fear of success. We'll cover self-assertiveness and self-motivation and look at ways to develop self-confidence. You'll also get an insight into what type of salesperson you are naturally.

All in your mind

You might still be reeling from the complexities of your prospect's mind that we uncovered in Chapter One. But that's nothing compared to what goes on in yours!

Selling is all in your mind. You've probably heard of the winning edge theory, which says that a small difference of maybe just 1 per cent in performance or attitude could be the difference between first and second place. And the difference between first and second place could be the difference between a sale or not. Well, how you feel about selling will determine what you do and how you do it, and ultimately will determine your success.

It will also determine how many of the recommendations in this book, or any other sales guide, you are prepared to try. So when you feel yourself dismissing something as you read it, ask yourself why you are so certain it won't work. Don't let your own beliefs and limitations prevent you from achieving the success you deserve.

Is it all right to want to be rich and successful, and to run a business that you enjoy? It seems quite a British peculiarity to associate negative connotations with wealth. But, if it's acceptable to provide employment, improve customers' lives, feel proud of what you do and want more of it, then it's all right to aspire to personal success.

You may have no aspirations to grow your business into a multi-national conglomerate, and that's absolutely your choice. That's certainly not what I envision for myself. But don't confuse that with thinking you have to struggle and scrape every day of your business life.

The obstacles

There are only really two obstacles to selling. One is the prospect's natural fear of making a mistake. The other is the seller's fear of rejection. You can take control and put right both of them. The trick is to stay with it long enough to get the first few winning experiences under your belt to raise your self-esteem and watch the cycle begin.

Prospects are on autopilot, they are so used to being sold to. Bring them back to life with the entrepreneurial sales approach and make them think. Use your humour and personality to say things they don't expect. This could even include being upfront about your nervousness, if you can find a subtle, comfortable way to include it!

Remember, you are working on your sales only when you are in direct contact with a real, live prospect or customer. You are not selling when you're filling out forms, writing proposals or stuffing direct mail envelopes. I know you're probably wondering about your new seven-stage sales process, but at least five of those stages should operate without you, so that you can focus on really selling.

The major time wasters often are procrastination and delay, putting off getting out there and talking to people. People who aren't making money in selling aren't talking to enough people. You should be aiming to spend 75–80 per cent of your time prospecting and pitching until you become too busy seeing customers.

Time saver

You could find your time draining away when you waste time with someone who's just waiting for a polite way to say no. When do you want a 'no'? Now! You have a business to run and dreams to achieve – don't waste your time and effort with prospects who don't deserve it, especially when there are plenty of others out there with real money, need and interest.

One of the biggest problems salespeople have is managing their time efficiently. You can increase your sales effectiveness by using your time to maximum efficiency. Advance planning is essential (discussed in detail in Chapter Seven), and you should plan every day in advance as part of your bigger plan. Schedule your first appointments and sales activities early in the day.

Your relationship to failure

If the selling process is turning out to be harder than it sounds, it could be you that's getting in the way of your own sales. What do I mean? I mean, you're staying in your comfort zone!

We spend many years and countless hours learning things in school and taking refresher courses in adulthood. Yet, when someone or something doesn't succeed as planned, it is a truly enlightened individual that remembers to label it for what it is – a learning experience. People who are able to recognise this when it shows up in their own lives are able to use it to their advantage. In fact, they are typically very successful because they possess a 'willingness to fail'. They're able to look at what most would consider a failure as a means to get to their final destination. Just because they go off-track temporarily does not mean they are not even closer to their target. It is simply targeting, realigning and targeting again until whatever they are after is achieved.

If fear of failure is keeping you from attempting something you long to do, ask yourself why you are letting it worry you. Is not taking a chance by doing something much more courageous than doing nothing at all? If everyone thought of failure as a major obstacle, we would not have the technological advancements that we are currently so accustomed to. We would still be in the Dark Ages if all those inventors, scientists and others had refused to step out of their comfort zones and dared to take a chance at failure. Isn't it time you made your mark? Is your passion for your business strong enough to inspire you?

Failure is just one step in the right direction to the ultimate goal of growth and success. Don't be afraid to try new things, stretch beyond your comfortable limits and stray off-course.

Questions that can move you forward

What are your sales goals?

Do you have a quota you need to meet? Are you trying to get your product into more retail outlets? Do you want more new customers or more repeat sales to existing customers? Are you trying to break into a new industry or territory? Is it more important to push a new product or revive a sagging performer in your line? Do you want to move cheap stuff or big-ticket items? How many suspects will you need to talk to in order to reach enough prospects? And how many prospects will you need to see to find enough paying customers?

Be specific, with numbers and dates. When you know exactly what you want to accomplish, it's easier to do it, because your goals will help define other aspects of your plan. If you can't quite put your finger on the answer, look at other companies – big and small, local and national – and see who you aspire to emulate.

Who are your ideal prospects?

This is a critical question, and I'll give you a hint: 'everyone' is the wrong answer! Most salespeople waste a majority of their time with prospects who will never do business with them. To maximise your prospecting time, you want to spend it with the people who are most likely to buy from you. This means you need to determine who your ideal prospects are. Who are the people who most need your products and will most appreciate their unique benefits?

Start your profiling by examining your current customers. What do they have in common? Then decide who else you want to target and list their defining characteristics. This chart can help:

If you're selling to businesses, possible characteristics might include:	If you're targeting consumers, possible characteristics might include:
Industry	Age
Type of business (manufacturing, retail, service, etc.)	Sex
Geographic location	Hobbies and lifestyle

▶

If you're selling to businesses, possible characteristics might include:	If you're targeting consumers, possible characteristics might include:
For-profit vs not-for-profit	Income
Private vs public sector	Profession
Annual revenue	Education level
Number of employees	Marital status
Customer profile	Number of children
Employee role profile	Age of children
Number of premises	Health status
Fleet of vehicles	Leisure activities

The more narrowly you can define your target prospect, the more effectively you can craft a sales proposition that resonates with them. After all, a three-person rural non-profit organisation has very different PC software needs from a multimillion-pound corporation.

Defining your ideal prospect doesn't mean that you will ignore everyone else – you'll probably still happily serve someone who doesn't happen to fit your profile. But your ideal prospects are the people you want to devote most of your time and energy to, because they are the ones who will provide you with the best return on your efforts.

Where are your best prospects?

Whoever your ideal prospects are, you'll probably find some of them everywhere. But you want to focus your efforts where the greatest concentrations of them are. We're not talking about just where people are physically located. You might also want to know what business events they go to, where they go for fun, what they read, what they watch and what they listen to. The more you know about where your ideal prospects are and what they do, the easier it is to figure out the answer to the next question.

How will you reach them?

You have dozens of prospecting tools at your disposal, including:

- → networking;
- → direct mail letters and mailers;
- → postcards;
- → Yellow Pages;
- → email (directly or through bought lists);
- → phone calls;
- → walk-in visits;
- → newspaper adverts;
- → magazine adverts;
- → press releases;
- → event sponsorships;
- → signs;
- → trade shows;
- → seminars;
- → focus groups;
- → online adverts;
- → special events;
- → referrals.

We'll cover tips for all of these throughout the book.

What is your hook?

Here's an important secret about sales in general and prospecting in particular – nobody cares about you, your company or your products. If you try to open with a sales pitch or by shoving a bunch of sales material into the hands of a prospect, you're wasting your time.

What people really care about is themselves. So lead with a hook instead of a pitch. A hook is something that is of value to the prospect and requires no effort, expense or risk on their part. Its purpose is to grab their attention and create a sense of perceived value and appreciation. A hook will radically improve your chances of securing an appointment to talk further with the prospect.

What is it worth?

Often, people don't buy on price. If we did, we'd all be driving the cheapest car and buying the cheapest food. And yet BMW, Waitrose and Selfridges all still make money.

The difference is in selling the value. If you don't give your customers any other information, all they can possibly do is compare prices. But once you make the invisible visible, they start to understand how your products and services meet their needs better than anyone else's offering. And this comes back to the age-old point, 'Why should your customers buy from you?'

This is not just about customers; this is good entrepreneurial business sense, too. Pricing decisions have a huge impact on the bottom line. The impact of a 10 per cent discount on a 30 per cent gross profit margin means that you would have to sell 50 per cent more to achieve the same overall total. At a 30 per cent gross profit margin, you could afford to lose 25 per cent of your customers if you introduced a 10 per cent price increase, with no loss of revenue.

So, a product selling at £100 RRP (recommended retail price), with a 30 per cent gross profit margin, gives you £30 profit per sale. A 10 per cent price reduction reduces your profit margin to £20, meaning 50 per cent more sales would be required to make up the difference.

Most businesses can usually sustain a 10 per cent price increase if the value of their offering is clearly stated. And by adding in guarantees and irresistible offers, price becomes even less of an issue. Ultimately, however, only your customers will decide what price they are prepared to pay.

Danger!

Most businesspeople don't charge what they're worth because their mindset tells them they can't. It would be outside their comfort zone. And they don't believe that people would pay it: 'If I put my prices up, my customers will just go somewhere cheaper.'

The steps to value

The three steps to success in this context are:

1 Believe in yourself.
2 Offer the right products to the right market.
3 Sell the value.

At the time of writing, the UK, and in fact the global economy, is in recession. And it's true that times are changing. But times are always changing. There are still business transactions taking place every day, everywhere in the world.

Being great at business means being able to set yourself apart from the rest, create long-term relationships with your customers and ultimately set your price. A great way to trial this on a smaller scale is to introduce a high-end range or move towards exclusive markets through your positioning and advertising. And remember, it's not a free price increase. You have to offer more in value than you charge in price.

Keep going!

Staying motivated is a struggle, and our drive is constantly assaulted by negative thoughts and anxiety about the future. Everyone faces doubt and uncertainty. What separates the highly successful entrepreneur is the ability to keep moving forward.

There is no simple solution for a lack of motivation. Even after beating it, the problem can reappear at the first sign of failure. The key is understanding your thoughts and how they drive your emotions. By learning how to nurture motivating thoughts, neutralise negative ones and focus on the task at hand, you can pull yourself out of a slump before it gains momentum.

There are three primary reasons we lose motivation:

1 Lack of confidence: if you don't believe you can succeed, what's the point in trying? Confidence and belief can permeate your business and your products, and conversely so can lack of confidence and lack of belief.

2 Lack of focus: if you don't know what you want, do you really want anything?

3 Lack of direction: if you don't know what to do, how can you be motivated to do it?

Building confidence

The first motivation killer is a lack of confidence. This creates negative thoughts. Past failures, bad breaks and personal weaknesses dominate your mind. You become jealous of your competitors and start making excuses for why you can't succeed. In this state, you tend to make a bad impression, assume the worst about others and lose self-confidence.

It might sound strange that repeating things you already know can improve your mindset, but it's amazingly effective. The mind doesn't filter for itself, so it distorts reality to confirm what you've stated is true. The more negatively you think, the more examples your mind will discover to confirm that belief. When you truly believe that you deserve success, your mind will generate ways to achieve it. The best way to bring success to yourself is to genuinely desire to create value for your customers, suppliers, partners and employees.

Focus overcomes fears

The second motivation killer is a lack of focus. How often do you focus on what you don't want, rather than on a concrete goal? We normally think in terms of fear. What if I end up poor? What if no one respects me? What if I end up alone? The problem with this type of thinking is that fear alone isn't actionable. Instead of doing something about our fear, it feeds on itself and drains our motivation.

If you're caught up in fear-based thinking, the first step is to focus that energy on a well-defined goal. By defining a goal, you automatically define a set of actions. If you have a fear of poverty, create a plan to increase your income. It could be going back to college, launching brave new products for your business or developing a profitable website. The key is moving from an intangible desire to concrete, measurable steps.

By focusing your mind on a positive goal instead of a general fear, you put your brain to work. It instantly begins devising a plan for

success. Instead of worrying about the future you start to ⊂
about it. This is the first step in motivating yourself to take
you know what you want, you become motivated to take a
like to find a complete programme for doing this, see
Power of Targeted Thinking by Jurgen Wolff (Pearson Education).

> ## If you don't see yourself as a winner, then you cannot perform as a winner. ZIG ZIGLAR

Direction gives you drive

The final piece in the motivational puzzle is direction. If focus means
having an ultimate goal, direction is having a day-to-day strategy to
achieve it. A lack of direction kills motivation, because without an obvious next action we succumb to procrastination. The key to finding
direction is identifying the activities that lead to success. For every
goal, there are activities that pay off and ones that don't. Make a list of
all your activities and arrange them based on results. Then make an
action plan that focuses on the activities that lead to big returns.

Regain direction by creating a plan that contains two positive
actions. The first one should be a small task you've been meaning to
do, while the second should be a long-term goal. Immediately do the
smaller task. This creates positive momentum. Then take the first step
towards achieving the long-term goal. Doing this periodically is great
for getting out of a slump, creating positive reinforcement and getting
long-term plans moving.

It's inevitable that you'll encounter periods of low energy, bad luck
and even the occasional disappointment. If you don't discipline your
mind, these minor bumps can turn into mental mountains.

Twenty steps to motivation

Keeping yourself motivated can be tough. Acknowledge the milestones
you achieve along the way. They might not mean much to anyone else,
but highlighting them to yourself is a huge way to ensure they don't slip
by unnoticed. Below are twenty steps to getting and staying highly

notivated for sales. Keep this list handy and refer to it if you start to feel your motivation flagging, or use it as a guide for ongoing personal development.

1 *Recognise that behaviour creates attitude.* Commonly held belief suggests that a positive mindset is required to act differently, but actually the opposite is true. Do what needs to be done and you will begin to feel the way you need to feel.

2 *Don't believe your eyes – or your ears.* Mental filters help us make quick decisions about common situations, but they also limit our potential to see things in a new light. Ask yourself good quality questions like, 'What else could this mean?'

3 *Don't beat yourself up.* Separate you as a person from you as a seller. You can be a great salesperson *and* a nice person; the two things aren't mutually exclusive.

4 *Figure out who you are.* Learn as much as you possibly can about who you are and why you think and feel the way you do. Self-knowledge is a key to success.

5 *Decide what you can and can't control.* Change and act on the things that are in your control and release the things that are out of your control.

6 *Accept responsibility.* Finding self-confidence requires accepting responsibility for your own happiness, as well as recognising that you are a product not only of your genetic code and your environment, but also of the choices you make.

7 *Make anxiety your ally.* Write down your worries for 30 days. Nagging concerns that loom so large in your imagination lose their power on paper. Amazingly, after writing them they'll begin to fade.

8 *Recognise that mistakes are opportunities.* Corny, but true. Keep the setback in perspective. Most mistakes are not personal tragedies. They are problems you now have the opportunity to solve. 'Success' is often a string of failed attempts to get it right.

9 *Compete to improve yourself, not to beat someone else.*

10 *Be ambitious.* When setting goals, remember that you are distinct from what you have and what you seem to be. If you let others

Selling for Entrepreneurs

define who you are, you may not find happiness. Pursue your own dreams.

11 *Be brave and take risks*. Don't be afraid of mistakes. Risk-taking builds confidence. When considering any risk, define a clear goal. Review the positive, practical and potential losses. Determine whether the risk is one of trust, identity, money, pride or some other factor. When you focus on risks that have a larger purpose, you can't go wrong. Even if the risk doesn't turn out as you hoped it would, you will gain from it.

12 *Make a decision*. The next time you ponder a decision, think of everything that could go right and say to yourself, 'What do I really have to lose?'

13 *Smile and be polite*. Use the words please and thank you consistently.

14 *Keep good company*. Positive feeds positive and negative breeds negative. If you choose to be around positive people you in turn will become more positive. It's said that you become like the people you associate with, and there's something in that, because you start to believe in their goals and aspirations.

15 *Reward yourself*. Give yourself and others rewards for being positive and doing well. If I've climbed a particularly steep hill, like writing this manuscript, I send myself a little card through the post, properly addressed to myself, wishing me congratulations. It might be too unspeakably twee for you even to consider this technique, but be sure to find a way of rewarding yourself.

16 *Don't accept messages that damage your own self-esteem*. It is much easier to improve or change your behaviour when you believe you are lovable and capable.

17 *Listen to messages*. Be aware of the different messages that you hear in your head. Remember to turn up the volume on the messages that contribute to your positive self-esteem and to turn down the volume on any message that encourages you to think negatively about your worth or ability.

18 *A small success can bring big feelings of competence*. Small steps lead to more steps. Pat yourself on the back every time you make a small success. Every step counts. Take one step at a time in a positive direction.

19 *Educate your customers*. If you don't tell them the value, they can only judge on the price. Eighty per cent of your profits may come from just 20 per cent of your customers and 80 per cent of your sales may come from just 20 per cent of your products and services. Talk passionately to customers about how you can help them.

20 *Examine how you feel*. How you feel determines how you sell, and knowing why you feel a certain way means you can choose to feel differently. Self-reliance and self-confidence mean you can do what your customer wants, not just what your competitors do.

Web bonus

At our website, **www.forentrepreneursbooks.com**, click on the 'Selling for Entrepreneurs' button. On the link for Chapter Two you'll find the Twenty Steps to Motivation, with extra try-them-now booster tactics.

Key points

→ Selling is all in the mind. Fear, apprehension, shyness and discomfort are all signals that our prospects pick up, which in turn creates doubt in their mind.

→ Fear of rejection can keep us chasing prospects that have no real interest, rather than simply giving them clear opportunities to say no.

→ Failure is only achieved by giving up. Knock-backs and disappointments can be positive learning experiences on the road to success.

→ The number and variety of techniques and methods you employ to sell to prospects and customers will depend on how you feel about selling.

→ Most businesses don't charge enough, simply through fear of the competition.

→ Keep yourself motivated and focused by creating detailed plans with specific goals.

→ Acknowledge the milestones you achieve along the way, even if no one else does.

Next steps

What action will you take to apply the information in this chapter? By when will you do it?

_____

_____

_____

_____

What are you selling?

Chapter Three

What is the most important thing that *really* sets your apart for your customers?

For example, there are many sellers out there who promote their low prices. This is fine... as long as they can sustain low costs.

Price could possibly be your USP, but only if you're the most expensive. Great companies (which yours undoubtedly is) providing great products and services (need I ask?) and benefiting their customers every way they look couldn't possibly be the cheapest in the market. And if you are, you're missing an opportunity to make lots more profit.

If today's economy is teaching us anything, it's that sustainability is vital. The other fundamental strategy is 'differentiation'. This simply means standing out from the crowd. So, rather than pricing up your products for the discount bin, you should really be asking, 'What is my USP?' And once you know your real USP, there are many things that you can do to make your enterprise stand out.

Know your customer

What does your product or service mean to your customer? Where does it fit in their life? How do they feel about it? How do they feel about you? How do you want them to feel?

Even the most well-segmented group of customers aren't all the same. Some are more important than others and some cost you more than others. Knowing which customers are the most profitable helps in a number of ways:

→ You can make sure you are really looking after those customers.

→ You can understand what it is about them that is making them profitable.

→ You can use that information to go out and find other customers who are like them.

→ You can gradually build up the number of profitable customers and reduce the number of less profitable ones.

You probably already have a hunch about which of your existing customers are worth the most to you, and you can become clearer on the types of relationship you want to replicate. Your entrepreneurial spirit might already be thinking about how much you're prepared to spend to get those customers through your door, by 'buying' them with the initial sale or a percentage of it, and thereby reducing all the risk in your business activity.

Competitive advantage

Providing first-class customer service is the most important differentiation your business can aspire to. Customers demand more from less and they don't even tell you. It's never been more important to learn this if you want to achieve targets, fend off competitors and nurture a more successful business.

If you're looking for the ultimate competitive advantage, customer service is by far the most consistently successful and the most difficult element for competitors to replicate. And who is your competitor? Everyone!

The goal of customer service is customer satisfaction. Customer satisfaction is what the customer feels subjectively and sometimes irrationally. There is all the difference in the world between a customer being satisfied and being not dissatisfied.

In fact, most businesses would be quite happy if their customers scored them five or six out of seven on satisfaction surveys. But a very comprehensive piece of research by Xerox showed that these customers were five times more likely to go to a competitor than a customer scoring a completely satisfied seven. Not getting complaints doesn't mean that you're providing the best service. Adore the customer who gives you honest feedback. They may well be speaking for half a dozen customers who feel the same way but will go elsewhere rather than tell you.

Have you ever done a customer survey, or obtained any formalised feedback from your customers? Maybe it's the time to start!

What are you doing?

Consider the following questions in order to analyse how well you are dealing with customers currently – how well you are understanding them, educating them, making it easy for them to buy from you. The rest of this book will help you to come up with answers that lead to more sales.

Do you understand the needs of your target audience?

The less you have to spend on your business, the more intimately you need to know your customers, because you can't afford to waste any money. Do they already get your product or service from elsewhere? Are they looking for someone more reliable/cheaper/quicker/more professional? If they don't already use your offering, do they understand why they should?

Do you focus all your business communications on your well-segmented intended audience?

Unless your intended audience want or need what you offer, you'll be fighting a losing battle from the start.

Do you always tell your customers the reasons 'why'?

Why should they buy from you instead of someone else? Why will your products and services meet their needs more effectively? Why are you running special offers or discounts? Why do you charge for returns? Why is something free?

Do you make it easy and appealing to do business with you?

Although your internal processes are valuable and important to you, if they make it difficult for customers to buy from you, they are ultimately harming your business. Do you really need forms filled? Are your special offers too complicated?

Do you test and measure the effectiveness of your business?

By testing, you'll have a really clear idea of what your audience responds to and you'll never waste money. In your copy you should try different headlines, a different PS, different offers, different guarantees, different bonuses, until you find the one that gets the best results. Then constantly try to improve it. Your business is always going to have the same fixed costs, however many leads it generates, so you owe it to your business to get the best possible return on your investment.

Do you educate your customer to see the value instead of the price?

If you don't relate the benefits, they can only compare price. Sell the value of your offering in terms of customer benefits.

Do you run direct response advertising?

You should only *ever* put your money into direct response advertising – that is, a specific offer requiring customers to take a certain action in order to learn more/grab the special deal or whatever the hook is. Advertising just to make them vaguely aware of your company is a waste – you have to make them phone/email/visit a website or whatever it is that you want them to do. It usually takes seven business communications from your company before people take *any* action at all. As we saw in Chapter One, your role is to help customers work through all the stages of the funnel.

In other words

Direct response advertising means adverts with very specific actions required of the reader or viewer, in contrast to 'brand' advertising, which is designed to build brand loyalty through emotions rather than boosting sales with specific actions.

Do you offer a back-end of products and services?

One-off sales equal the constant, risky, expensive search for new customers. By understanding what else your customers buy, you can ensure a constant stream of sales. This is not only good business sense for you, but it also shows your customers that you really understand them and their needs.

Do you develop campaigns that are already working?

Don't stop doing anything that works, no matter how bored you are by it. Try to constantly improve instead, using the following strategies.

Focus on benefits and understand value

Focus on the benefits and understand the value you provide to your customers. The only way to do this completely is to ask, 'What are their needs and how do we solve them?' Even if you think you know, ask a handful of your customers. You can never know too much about why people buy from you. They don't care how long you've been in business or how many staff you employ. They care what you can do for them. Benefits build rapport by demonstrating that you understand their point of view. If customers are saying 'it's too expensive', they haven't understood the value of your offering.

Understand customer lifetime value

By understanding customer lifetime value, you understand the total value of a customer to your business. When you understand how much a customer is worth to you, you can fully understand the cost of acquisition and conversion, and decide how much cash and time you want to dedicate to them.

In other words

Customer lifetime value is the total value of your customers during the whole time that they buy from you.

Provide explicit guarantees

By providing explicit guarantees, you remove obstacles to sale. It's vital that your customers view you more distinctively or advantageously than your competition. And to do this, you can make it your responsibility to allow customers to preview and experience your offering, entirely at your risk. Every business really guarantees the sales transaction, through standard practice or legal obligation. But they brush it under the carpet rather than highlight the benefits of this for the customer.

By making the guarantee a powerful condition of sale, you can state specifically how the customer will come out protected and ahead of the game. Imagine from your customers' perspective the choice of suppliers available to them. Four other businesses might not mention their guarantees, or might state it is a basic legal requirement. But you not only mention it, you also insist that it be a condition of doing business. Which supplier would you choose? It might seem too daunting to provide guarantees for every element of your offering, but everything that performs at the level you promise can be guaranteed in some way.

Keep communicating

Keep communicating by educating, informing and entertaining. Position yourself as an expert to gain your customers' trust and confidence, through your PR, direct communications and your website. Provide information, reviews, reports or details on your specialist area. Customers often don't know the right questions to ask, so help them out by anticipating their concerns and providing straight answers.

A closer look at your USP

A USP is one of the basics of effective marketing and business that has stood the test of time. It is the distinguishing advantage you state in all your marketing, advertising and sales. You must distinguish yourself within your market. And you should stand up and be proud of the things that differentiate your business from all the others.

We spend lots of time and money distinguishing our business from our competitors with our branding, our website, our offers and prices, even our delivery capabilities. And yet, a USP is free to create!

Why did you set up in this business? What can you do better or quicker than the competition? Why should customers want to buy from you? This is almost *never* exclusively about price. Even if your prices are low, it is more likely to be the variety of products or the speed of delivery that forms your USP. Are you one of the huge majority of companies who don't have a clear USP and muddle along in the middle ground defending their prices?

What could you proudly say sets you apart from everyone else in your field and, more importantly, puts you into the top 1 per cent of buying experiences that your customers have in their daily lives? Your USP could be a better guarantee, more reliable and efficient delivery or a handmade or unique element.

It's often a problem identifying our USP when we start our own businesses, because we know everything about our product or service, so that's what we want to talk about. But, in the nicest possible way, customers don't care. They care that it will make them richer, more successful, less stressed, more attractive and so on. So creating a USP is going to be a big part of getting into your customer's mindset.

 Never say anything about yourself you do not want to come true. BRIAN TRACY

One USP or many?

As we've seen, a USP can help customers by saving them time when they are considering buying a product or service, and when you state simply and clearly why your product or service is different, it will stand out from the competition. You can create different USPs for every product or service in your range, if appropriate, or you can create a company-level USP, focusing on your incredible customer service or technological investments, for example.

Every business needs a USP for its products and services. We are faced every day with over 3,000 sales and business messages – to stand out in this crowded marketplace, you must be better, faster, cheaper, nicer or more exclusive than your competitors. If you're a re-seller of someone else's products, or a central point for the products of a number of different suppliers, how do you offer something unique? How can you expand on the offer of the manufacturers themselves?

Why would people be interested if your proposition is no different from your competition? Emphasise what makes your service special and new. Unless your code of practice prevents you from claiming superiority over your competitors, you should put as much emphasis as you can behind your USP, and either imply or state directly that you are the only company to offer these things. How you feel about yourself, your product and selling in general could affect how dynamic and ambitious your USP is.

The process of identifying a USP helps you to focus on the key benefits that help to sell your products or services. And, as I'm sure you know by now, the three key areas for focus in business are benefits, benefits, benefits!

Keep educating customers about why you are so special. Once you've told them, tell them again, as I've done in this section – in this case, I'm selling you the importance of your USP by explaining what it will do for you.

Customer relationships

Your customer relationships are vital to any plans and desires you have for your business. There are three finite ways to grow a business. You must:

1 Get new customers.

2 Increase the average sale value every time customers buy from you.

3 Increase the frequency that customers purchase, either the main product or service you sell, or by offering a diverse range of back-end and related products that need to be replaced more often.

Ideally, you should be looking to do a combination of all three.

Excellent customer service means less focus on acquiring new customers (1), who are notoriously costly in time and money, and more focus on quality relationships with profitable customers (2) and (3).

The role of customer service

Excellence in customer service can help you to retain customers. This means:

→ They are less likely to go to your competitors in the increasingly competitive markets where customers have more choice than ever.

→ As satisfied customers, they will recommend you to others, resulting in an increase in new business. It is said that it costs up to ten times as much to win a new customer as to keep an existing one.

→ They are more forgiving and less likely to tell other people of bad experiences. Customers experiencing poor service are likely to tell up to 20 people about their experience, which is not a good advertisement for your business. This may deter others from even trying you out, and so you will not get the chance to impress them, even with the best or most innovative products and services.

→ By focusing your attention on the customers that have the highest potential lifetime value, you can improve profitability.

→ Your staff will have a feelgood factor because of the environment and atmosphere that creates happy customers. This can help to attract additional new staff and customers over time.

What customers want

Customers don't compare like with like any more. They compare experience with experience. This could include:

→ the company that picks up the phone quicker;

→ the company that delivers an order faster;

→ the company that exceeds expectations more regularly;

→ the company that understands customer needs more clearly.

Research has shown repeatedly that there are three secrets to getting business referrals, and all of them are reliant on your staff delivering the quality service you need. The three elements are:

1 Always doing what you say you will.

2 Being on time.

3 Always saying please and thank you.

If those sound unbelievably simplistic, they are! And that is why they are constantly overlooked or forgotten.

Tips for customer service

Here are some simple strategies for providing good customer service:

→ Involve the whole of your team in setting service standards.

→ Include the personal dimensions of customer service in standards such as appearance, body language, tone of voice, tact, advice given, problem solving approach used, attentiveness and so on.

→ Deliver a personalised service wherever possible. Train staff to use the customer's name in all communications with them.

→ Train all employees in communication skills and to handle customer complaints positively. Complaints should be considered opportunities to keep a customer by changing something to improve customer service.

→ Rate the behaviour of your customer service staff in each of the above areas and give training where appropriate.

→ Consider rewarding staff for significant contributions to customer service. Rewards do not need to be costly, but, once a programme is in place, it must be maintained to be meaningful and credible.

Your turn: define your USP

Let's look at a three-step process for identifying your USP – the factor that is going to help you win and keep your customers. Set aside at least half a day to do this exercise. Gather together a team of people to help you. If you're a sole trader, this might be a great activity to do with some other, non-competing entrepreneurs.

You will need several large sheets of paper. You start by writing down the following question: 'Why do our customers buy from us?'

As the session progresses, your job as facilitator is to probe deeper and deeper to find out the real reasons why people buy from you. Socrates would never accept the first answer that people gave him. He kept on saying, 'Yes, but why is this the case?' If you do this in a consistent, non-confrontational way, you will be amazed at what your team comes up with. You need to deepen your understanding to cover all your products and services in all of the vertical, geographic and other markets that you sell to.

The second step, in the second half of the session, is to ask the question, 'Why do companies buy from other sources?' As before, keep questioning until you uncover some high-quality answers. If you really struggle with this stage, it might be a great opportunity to ask some of your best customers about the reasons behind their buying decisions.

Step three is to cancel out the ideas/answers that are the same for your company and the competition.

At the end of the session, the answers that remain for your enterprise will reveal your true USP. If you still don't have one, this is a good time to start thinking about creating one.

Once you have decided what your USP is, distil the answers into one single corporate USP. Your mission then is to tell your prospects and clients about it.

Another USP process

Another way to create a unique USP is to follow these eleven steps:

1 Start with the features of your products or services.

2 Understand how and why your customers use them.

3 Identify features of your competitors' products or services.

4 Choose one product or service that is most profitable or you have most information about.

5 Write all the features down the left-hand side of a piece of paper.

6 Against each feature, on the right-hand side, write the benefit to the customer (an easy way to get into the mindset is to write 'which means that…' after the feature).

7 Rank the benefits in order of priority, based on your customers' needs.

8 Consider whether each benefit is standard in your industry or unique to you.

9 If the benefits are not unique, think about how you could develop your product or service features to deliver new customer benefits that are not provided by your competitors.

10 State your unique selling point(s) consistently in all your business communications.

11 No USP will last for ever. By constantly understanding your customer needs, you can keep your products and services at the forefront.

The key ingredient: customer service

How does your service compare to the experiences your customers have when they shop with Amazon? Or Waitrose? Or Timpsons? Or any of the other businesses who've made customer service their focus?

Outstanding service makes customers feel more special and loved, and also more forgiving. Conversely, unhappy and stressed customers buy a lot less. So, increasing the level of your customer service will ensure your customers feel more inclined to spend money whilst making them more likely to overlook any problems. And really incredible service usually costs little or nothing – what a perfect combination! Make the whole experience of dealing with you fabulous (and relevant to your audience and the total value of your product or service) and you also remove a lot of objections and barriers to sales.

Your internal customer is just as important as your external customer. Happy staff provide superior customer service, so treat your staff the way you want them to treat your customers.

You know you want it, you know it will be incredibly valuable to your business and you know your customers deserve it. But how do you achieve it? What are the elusive elements of customer service that put some businesses leagues ahead of their competitors? They follow these golden rules to stay constantly customer focused:

→ Focus on the benefits and understand the value you provide to your customers.

→ Understand how much a customer is worth to you.

→ Provide explicit guarantees, which remove obstacles to sale.

→ Keep communicating by educating, informing and entertaining.

You'll recognise these points from pages 44–5, where we looked at them in more detail – refer back to those pages to reinforce your understanding.

In addition to the above points, the layout of the store or website, the tone of the person serving us and the ease of the purchase can make all the difference between a slightly daunting experience and a truly horrible situation we never want to repeat.

Equally, a shop or office that is well laid out and uses appropriate music and technology can offer a pleasant experience. Selfridges is a good example of a USP above other department stores, because they've identified their audience as young urban professionals, and they offer food samples, an in-store DJ and a lively, young, urban experience.

Don't assume that not getting complaints means that you're providing the best service

Appreciate the customer who gives you honest feedback. They may well be speaking for half a dozen customers who feel the same way but will go elsewhere rather than tell you.

Weaknesses and gaps in customer service can occur between delivery, perception and expectation, and resolving issues may be as simple as understanding what your customer expected from you in the first place.

How to do it

Here are some methods you can use to ensure that you are delivering the customer experience that will keep them coming back:

→ Involve customers and staff in developing the standards.

→ State standards clearly and document them.

→ Ensure all standards link to company goals.

→ Check them back against your survey findings.

→ Make all standards achievable and easy to understand.

→ Make sure all standards and the programme have the support of all your management team.

→ Communicate standards clearly to all involved on an ongoing basis.

→ Once the standards are established, develop a culture in which deviation from the standards becomes unacceptable.

→ Review standards on a systematic basis to make sure they are still relevant and appropriate.

→ Add new standards as necessary, with the full approval of all staff involved in delivery.

Toolkit

If you're ready for a real insight into excellent customer service, I recommend Michael Heppell's *Five Star Service, One Star Budget*, published by Prentice Hall and **www.mycustomer.com** – the voice of the customer relationship management profession, which offers useful blogs and podcasts.

Key points

→ As well as the products and services your business provides, what qualities and benefits do you sell? These are what your customer really buys.

→ How you price your products and services is a huge reflection of your own belief and the value you feel they provide to your customers.

- → By segmenting your customers, you will be able to target the right benefits to the right group, and identify the groups that are most beneficial for your business, in time and money.

- → Understanding your customer groups doesn't have to be expensive, but it is a very important investment for every business.

- → A unique selling point is probably the cheapest sales tool you'll ever use, but one that takes the most intensive thought.

- → Your competitors aren't just the other businesses who sell the same products and services as you. They are every sales interaction your customers have in their day.

Next steps

What action will you take to apply the information in this chapter? By when will you do it?

_____

_____

_____

_____

The sales process

Part Two

Prospecting for opportunities

Chapter Four

Prospecting means getting your metaphorical sieve and sifting through to find the nuggets of gold. However, as we've seen from the funnel that we first described in Chapter One, lumps of gold aren't money in the bank just yet … but they can be.

Prospecting includes telephone calls, scripts, lists, cold calling, mailing, face-to-face meetings and counter conversations, referrals, seminars, open days and demonstrations. Pitching – that is, presenting your business succinctly and dynamically – is another way to get prospects into the funnel, and is covered in detail in the next chapter.

Don't hide behind all the other prospecting tools – they're not sales – but they are all important stages in the process.

Cold calling can be, and is, a very effective way to prospect. But if you've suddenly come over all weak at the knees at the thought of it, your experience of cold calling might be a dose of rejection or, worse, the caller from hell who wouldn't take your subtle hints and leave you alone. Stick with it, my friend, and I promise you'll learn the entrepreneurial way to cold call and remain a nice person.

The first thing to say is that you don't have to force yourself to build your whole client list from cold calling. As we saw in Chapter Three, there are three ways to grow a business: get new customers; increase the average sale value every time customers buy from you; and increase the frequency that customers purchase. By focusing on all three you can achieve a cumulative triple effect that could equal 100 per cent growth.

Do any one of the three things and you can grow in a linear manner. Do any combination of the three and you can grow exponentially. Let's see how this works.

In other words

Prospecting is the sales process of searching out and communicating with potential or likely customers or clients.

Pitching is the sales process of succinctly explaining what your business does in a way that highlights the benefits to your customers.

Cold calling is making calls to individuals or companies that have no previous relationship with your business.

If you increase the number of customers by 10 per cent, the unit of sale by 10 per cent and the re-purchase frequency by 10 per cent, you could actually achieve 45 per cent growth. It's easier to be exponential than linear, and it's easier to grow quickly than grow slowly when you become proactive and increase your effectiveness in these areas.

If, for example, your turnover was £100,000, an average spend was £50 and customers purchased three times a year, you could achieve a 100 per cent increase by:

→ increasing new customers by 30 per cent @ £50 average annual spend = £30,000;

→ increasing average spend by 20 per cent from £50 to £60 = £25,000;

→ increasing times purchased from three to four per year = £50,000.

In business, a consistent multiple approach is always more effective.

Most businesses could even sustain a 10 per cent price increase if the value is clearly stated. Only your customers will decide what they are prepared to pay.

Of course, there will be a finite amount of times that you can educate customers to repeat their purchase of the same product or service every year, and a ceiling price that they will pay, but by increasing the back-end of your offer you can always provide them with new ways to meet their needs.

Limiting the attrition rate

For the funnel to work, you must also measure your attrition rate. That is, looking at how many prospects drop out at each stage and why. By improving your skills for getting the time-wasters out as quickly as possible, whilst also ensuring that those with genuine time, need and money are helped from one stage to the next, your prospecting efforts will keep your funnel populated with valuable opportunities. Don't accept a 'slow no' – there are plenty of people out there who want what you sell, so give a negative prospect every chance to back out gracefully as soon as possible.

Steve Wright, colleague and trainer extraordinaire with the Sandler Sales Institute, gives his class a fantastic line that builds confidence in you and the person you've just called. It goes like this: 'Your time is valuable and so is mine. I want to make sure we don't waste a single minute. I'm not sure yet if there's a fit between your needs and my products/services, but if we reach the point where it looks unlikely, are you comfortable saying so?' Isn't that great?

This regular communication with your customers and prospects throughout the prospecting process will obviously have an impact on sales, but it will also provide you with information about your audience's thoughts on pricing, products and communications. You can use that to reinforce and re-establish relationships.

That's not to say it's easy, though. Great companies know that things don't just fall in their laps. Direct mail and telephone sales, especially to prospects who have never bought from you before, are hard work. It takes time, and it means lots of testing, measuring, tweaking and improving.

Getting prospects to enjoy contact with you

At no point should any of your sales become high-pressure, pushy, aggressive hard sell. That does occasionally work for a tiny number of companies, but imagine how easy their lives would be if they mastered their prospecting and tried these techniques instead. And imagine how much more fun the whole sales process would be for them! The trick is to apply entrepreneurial thinking to these neglected strategies. You realise that working harder isn't going to move your business forward as much as you'd like. You know that being smarter and opening your mind to effective ideas will make the difference.

If you are building great relationships with your prospects and customers, they will like being contacted. They will appreciate being appreciated. And you might even be making their job easier, especially if they've been meaning to contact you.

Of course, you might end up speaking to one or two people who are just having a bad day. If you're prone to taking these things personally, remember the psychology of selling that says the sale is won or lost in the mind. Keep yourself motivated and focused.

Selling for Entrepreneurs

How many calls or letters have you received in the last week from companies with whom you have a good relationship? One? None? It's so rare as to be almost non-existent.

What a great opportunity! What if your hairdresser called a couple of days after your appointment to check you were happy? What about getting a letter from your local cinema offering you a chance to book opening-night tickets for a film they think you'd like? And what if you contacted your customers with great relationship-building follow-ups and related product offers as well?

Have you launched any new products or services recently? No? When you've created some great new ideas, contact your existing customer base and tell them all about it.

When you send out catalogues and price lists, do you include a covering letter selling the reasons why they should look through it? That's like walking into a presentation and starting the sales pitch without even introducing yourself!

There are so many offers and opportunities you can present to your customers and prospects without ever needing to give them the hard sell. Try different approaches and see what works for your audience. It could mean the difference between average results and exceptional business growth.

The nuts and bolts of prospecting

The first thing to do is to prepare your objectives for prospecting, and these must be measurable. What could you come away with after a first call? Do you want people to request further information? Are you trying to organise sales meetings? Or can you actually take orders over the phone?

At the very least, you should start with the organisation's name, the name and position of the person to contact, possible objections based on your knowledge of them, their key problems, the internal or available resources for solving the problem and time-scales for the solution.

The prospecting script

Below is an example of a prospecting script. I've used the scenario of an organisation offering IT training, but the principles are transferable to any situation. Note that since there are no answers to these questions (and, of course, answers often create the shape and direction of discussions), they are just an example of how the process works. In this case, the script consists of the following questions:

How do you currently train your people in IT?

How is that working for you?

Is anything missing?

Is there something further you'd want but aren't getting? What's stopping you from getting what you want from your IT training?

How are you set up to fix this problem with the current resources you've got in place (i.e. internal trainers)?

Is anything stopping you from using your current resources to fix the problem?

What would you need to know in order to consider doing something different from what you are currently doing in the area of IT training?

How will you know that whatever skills you decide to add will work with what you are currently doing, and you won't lose the success you've already attained?

What type of decision would you and your team need to make that's different from the one you made that brought you the training you are now running?

How do you plan on aligning the (management, partners, initiatives) so that if you decide to add new IT skills, they will be happy to work with you on the change?

What criteria would you need to have filled to understand that a different or alternative training approach would work alongside the approach you are currently using?

How would you know that a chosen provider or solution would meet those criteria?

How would you know we could deliver this and match your criteria?

In the context of your business, undoubtedly these are the kind of questions you discuss when you're comfortable with a prospect – so why not with every prospect?

Getting their attention

Your first contact with the prospect will begin the process that may or may not lead to a sale. Therefore, every word of your approach should be thought through in advance. You must get the prospect's attention and you will only have about 30 seconds to do this. Before the prospect will relax and listen to you, they want to be sure of five things:

1 You have something important to communicate.

2 You're talking to the right buyer.

3 Your visit or call will be short.

4 There will be no obligations.

5 There will be no pressure.

Don't wait for the phone to ring. You can source prospects and actively engage them from existing and lapsed customers including 'not today's', lapsed prospects, newspaper stories, job adverts, referrals, contacts and cold lists.

Time saver

Give prospects the opportunity to respond, but if they are not interested, move on quickly.

Telephone prospecting is always endorsed in sales books and training, and being good on the telephone is absolutely something you should be constantly trying to achieve. You can't avoid it. But calling cold suspect lists might not be right for you or your business. You won't know until you've tried. And I mean, really tried. For a period of time and to different segments in your customer list. As an employee, you might have had a prospect list provided for you as part of your territory, or within one of the company's systems. As an entrepreneur, it's up to you to create one.

You may want to start by using these methods as part of your after-sales process. By talking to people who are already your customers, you will gather useful information and gain confidence in your telephone manner.

How much prospecting is necessary?

How much do you want to earn? How many sales will you need to get to that margin? How many customers do you need to get to that amount of sales? How many prospects must you have to be able to convert enough into customers? How many appointments or phone calls or demos or mailers or other interaction with suspects do you need to get to that many prospects? We'll cover all these points in Chapter Seven on Managing your sales, but it is vital to be very clear on what you want and need to achieve.

One of the incredible things about telephone prospecting is the ability to target your audience with pinpoint precision. You can choose job title, geography, turnover, age, income, buying behaviour; a focus that even the best PR, advertising and online positioning can't hope to match.

There are complex mental decisions to be made during the buying process, and if you can't be with your prospects face to face, the telephone is the next best thing. Ask them questions, listen to their views, overcome their objections and ultimately influence their decision. And, at the same time, allow yourself the opportunity to overcome any generalisations you might have made about your customers and resolve assumptions you might identify about their buying behaviour or capacity for your offerings.

You may also want to consider augmenting this effort by adding direct mail as a tool. Print also engenders a kind of conversation. In a way, we're conversing now, you and I. As I write this, I'm thinking of specific clients, experiences and concepts that my business has advised on, and I'm sure sometimes you're agreeing with me, and sometimes not. But hopefully my questions and techniques are making you think about how they could work in your own business. Your powerful direct mail letters or flyers or catalogues can spark the same kind of response regarding your products or services.

When you send a direct mail campaign, you can increase your response by as much as 30 per cent by following up with a phone call.

In fact, some of the most successful campaigns use these two techniques in tandem.

There is only one thing that makes prosperity, and that is work. HENRY FORD

More reasons to be in touch

There's no need to stop at just trying to find new customers. What about telephone sales to old and inactive customers? Why don't they buy from you any more? Maybe they had a bad experience? Or things have changed and they no longer live near enough to your shop? Or maybe they moved over to your competitors? Reactivating old customers is one of the single most profitable ways to increase business in the short term. And what better way to do it than with a personal phone call to show how much they mean to you?

Also, have you thought of using telephone sales techniques to communicate with the media? When you send out your great press releases, you should be following up and chasing any hot leads and using the opportunity to get feedback.

Whilst it's true that nobody likes to be pestered at work, we all like getting phone calls or letters from people we like. Even if we're busy and unable to give them our full attention at that moment, it makes us smile momentarily to know they were thinking of us. It isn't a chore. It doesn't offend us.

Here is the absolute foundation, the golden rule, and the key principle of success in telephone sales and direct mail: be their friend. Offer them something useful and beneficial and exciting. When you finally reach that prospect or customer, make them feel special. If this is a special offer, a limited opportunity or something reserved just for your best customers, say so. And never, ever be boring! Boring mailers and routine phone calls will mean instant death to your campaign. No one wants to talk to a faceless robot reading from a script.

If you've bought in the data you're calling or mailing, be sure you are using lists less than two years old. Cheap lists have cheap, incorrect details and these will annoy your potential customers.

The rules of prospecting

The following list gives you a simple summary of what you need to do:

1 Find clusters of people/organisations with the same needs.
2 Find out as much as you can about their situation.
3 Create compelling propositions, which address their needs.
4 Differentiate yourself.
5 Use the promotional mix to communicate your proposition. Keep communicating – face to face, on the phone, by post and so on.

Cold calling in practice

We're now going to work through all the stages of cold calling.

First things first

Start by always setting targets for the number of calls and/or the number of decision maker conversations, or the number of 'successes' (appointments, direct sales, etc.) that you will achieve for each session. It is amazing what you can achieve, if you set yourself a target.

How do you ensure that you are working off a 'clean list'? In other words, how can you be sure that you have accurate data and that you won't constantly be told that 'Mr Smith no longer works here'. It is quite common for agencies to begin by calling an entire list, to check that the contact information is correct. This might be something you want to do yourself, or something you trust someone else to do on your behalf.

The whole thing is a process from research, through acquisition, customer service and business development. And throughout, you should be updating your database with all this mission-critical information.

What's your offer?

Are you making an offer on the phone? For example, you might be giving the person a chance to:

- → receive information in the post;
- → enter a prize draw;
- → make an appointment;
- → see a demonstration;
- → respond early to a promotion and receive a discount;
- → come to an event.

Your results will be much better if you make a specific offer. Just asking whether they are currently 'in the market' or whether they have heard of you is not nearly as powerful.

Part of the fun of business is coming up with lots of ideas for offers, so that you can hit on one or two great ones. How do you figure out which ones are the best? Test them out! When you've thought of several offers, test a number out on different subsets of your database. Then ramp up the one which produced the best result.

Should you use a script?

Scripts are a very useful tool to start the conversation going. In addition, scripts are something that you can test and change. It is staggering how a few minor changes to a script can double or treble response rates. But if you and your colleagues are all saying different things each time you call, how can you measure what is effective and what isn't? There will be some phrases that are very powerful for your audience and some that may turn them off. This is also true of every time someone comes to your shop counter.

I am not suggesting that you should read the script every time you make a call. Once you've used the script a few times, it will be like the lines that actors learn. You will have memorised it and you will be able to repeat it without actually reading it.

Use the right tone

When you're prospecting, always be polite, firm and respectful. Assure the prospect that there will be no high-pressure tactics – and mean it. Guard your integrity as sacred. Smile as you talk, relax and visualise yourself enjoying the whole experience. Pinpoint a date and time for the appointment, or a follow-up call if necessary. And always thank the prospect sincerely for their time, and confirm the date and time you've committed to.

If you have any reason to doubt that they're planning to take the appointment seriously, one great piece of advice I was given by a colleague, James Cash, a truly entrepreneurial salesman, was to set prospects a piece of homework to complete before the meeting. This should be something very easy, just requiring a few minutes of their time. But if they don't send it back before the meeting, you can make a judgement on how seriously they view the appointment.

The influence of a calm, confident, relaxed salesperson is very powerful. Professional salespeople actually have a very soothing effect. They exude confidence in themselves, their business and their products. They don't give the impression of being desperate for the sale; they make us work a little bit to be their prospect and we feel comfortable in conversation with them.

Personalise

We've talked about the need to focus on your customers as individuals, with their own wants and needs, and their own reasons for buying from you. You should always ensure that any lists you rent or buy have accurate contact details, perhaps even entered by the person themselves, if possible, so that you can address them accurately.

It is commonly held that repeating someone's name during a conversation builds rapport. Apparently this is based on the idea that it replicates a conversation between friends. Personally I find it uncomfortable and fake, but if you can use this tactic in a sincere and genuine way, it will help the caller or reader feel important. It is absolutely true that people love nothing more than their own name, so you get it wrong at your peril. If and when you use someone's name, make sure you get it right.

Ask permission

Show telephone prospects courtesy by asking their permission to continue the call. A simple 'Do you have a couple of minutes...?' is fine. If you're feeling confident and you have a good sense of humour, you could even say, 'This is a cold call, and I'd like to talk to you for three minutes. After that time, if we haven't established any reason to carry on talking, you can just put the phone down. How does that sound?'

Compel them

Whether you're communicating by post or phone, ensure that your offer is almost impossible to refuse. A good way to test this was suggested by Dan Kennedy, the American marketing guru. He said that no matter what you are selling, when you create the details of your offer, imagine the product or service is worth £15,000 (or another figure ten times the value of your product if it's already worth £15,000).

What bonuses, offers, guarantees and extras would you add to make £15,000 seem like a great price for your offering? Then try adding them.

Focus on benefits

Your customers don't care about you. They care about their own life, their problems, their ambitions and themselves. Focus your offer on the benefits it provides for them. And remember, it's really only a benefit if it solves an issue or adds value to something that the customer recognises as significant.

Deal with objections

Embrace the objections, don't try to avoid them. Chapter Six is dedicated to overcoming objections like 'I don't have time', 'I can't afford it' and 'I need to think about it'. So get your answers prepared and show prospects why they can't possibly afford to miss this great opportunity!

Create rapport

By matching the tone, volume and speed of the other person's voice, you will create an instant rapport and your prospect will feel more comfortable speaking to you. Obviously you have to do this in a subtle way, so they don't feel you are mocking them.

Remember to smile as you speak and keep your chin off your chest, as your caller will 'hear' that when you speak.

Surround yourself with great views, inspiring photos and rousing wise words – such as the quotations throughout this book – whatever it takes to ensure you keep the genuine passion and enthusiasm in your voice.

Ask questions

It is a common misconception that someone who makes calls on behalf of your company must know lots about your business. But the more they know about your business, the more they will feel inclined to talk about you. However, you know that customers care about themselves, not you. So the sign of a truly great entrepreneur is someone with exceptional communication skills. This means asking excellent questions and being genuinely interested in how to help the customer. You have to know what your prospect wants and why they want it before you can really tell them what you have.

Prospects won't answer your questions honestly unless they trust and respect you. If they won't talk, you can't sell; if you aren't listening, you can't sell.

Close

If the sale is in the customer's best interest, ask for it. Don't let your customers and prospects put down your mailer or end the phone call without being given a serious opportunity to benefit from your offering.

At the end of the call or mailer ask them, 'Shall I go ahead and book that/reserve that/arrange that for you?'

If they're ready to buy, stop talking. Sometimes salespeople keep talking past the time when they should be closing, and they talk themselves right out of a sale.

Overcome call reluctance

If you still have some doubts about cold calling, that's not unusual. Call reluctance is similar to self-confidence in that it fluctuates. No one is self-confident all of the time. Making sales calls takes proactive effort on your part and forces you out of your comfort zone. Here are some ways to make it easier:

Selling for Entrepreneurs

→ *Change your objective.* If, instead of aiming to make the sale, your objective is to discover whether there is an opportunity to be of service to this client, either now or in the future, then you will associate success with many more calls. Success breeds confidence.

→ *Have clear activity objectives with small rewards.* The first call is always the hardest, so you may want to set up small rewards to get going early. The best time to do sales calls is first thing in the morning before you get distracted.

→ *Fully believe in what you are selling.* In order to be effective you need to be completely sold on what you are selling. People always said of Anita Roddick, founder of The Body Shop, that her enthusiasm for her products was contagious.

→ *Choose prospects or companies that you feel good about calling.* Work in specialities that you feel passionate about so that you are excited about speaking to your prospects.

→ *Expect some rejection, then you won't be shocked and deflated when it occurs.* Just accept it as part of the process and don't let it throw you.

→ *Prospect in a way that fits with your values and personality.* Allow your quirks and sense of humour to come through. Don't be a robot.

→ *Have an 'accountability partner' or coach.* Buddy up with a co-worker or friend who can be your partner and to whom you will report your daily activity.

→ *Review your primary goals daily.* If you have a big enough 'Why' then the 'How' becomes much easier. What are your goals? How will they benefit you? Take a moment each day to feel the positive feelings of these goals coming to fruition.

If we all did the things we are capable of doing, we would literally astound ourselves.

THOMAS EDISON

Key points

→ Even the most confident seller can sometimes be intimidated by the amount of prospecting required to build up the necessary list of prospects for a business.

→ Prospecting tools make prospects aware of your business, and ideally begin the dialogue which helps you both decide whether it's worth progressing.

→ Growing your business significantly involves prospecting for brand new business, increasing business from existing customers, renewing the interest of lapsed customers and increasing frequency of sales.

→ Prospecting is a great way to build strong relationships with lots of audiences that are valuable to your business, including the media and potential partner companies.

→ Having clear objectives for your prospecting gives you the opportunity to celebrate more frequent successes than simply 'getting the sale'.

→ Always talk to your prospects like real people during your prospecting, and they'll usually do the same.

Next steps

What action will you take to apply the information in this chapter? By when will you do it?

_____

_____

_____

_____

Pitching your business

Chapter Five

Have you ever wasted an opportunity by floundering for a succinct, accurate answer to the question, 'So, what does your company do?'

One of the most important things a businessperson can do, especially an entrepreneur, is learn how to speak about their business to others. Being able to sum up unique aspects of your service or product in a way that excites others should be a fundamental skill. It's often referred to as pitching, and you must know it, rehearse it and be confident using it whenever you can. Be passionate. Be compelling.

Prospecting vs pitching

Prospecting and pitching have some elements in common, but also some differences. Here are the key aspects of both:

Prospecting includes:	Pitching includes:
Telephone calls to existing customers	Networking
Counter conversations	Public speaking
Face-to-face meetings	Hosting events
Cold calling	Elevator pitches
Email campaigns	Running personal consultations
Telephone calls to lapsed customers	Customer hospitality
Direct mail	30-second commercials
Referral opportunities	Presentations and client pitches
Postcards	Speaking at exhibitions or trade events
	Hosting workshops
	Radio and television appearances
	Stadium pitches

We looked at prospecting in detail in Chapter Four; now we will explore pitching.

The elevator pitch

An elevator pitch is so named because it shouldn't last longer than an average lift ride. It's also known as a 30-second commercial. It's brief, but it is far too important to take casually. It's one of the most effective methods available to reach new buyers and clients with a winning message. True, you'll rarely be doing the pitching in an actual lift, but even if your meeting is a planned, sit-down event, you should still be prepared to capture your audience's attention quickly.

An elevator pitch is one of the most useful tools you can have in your small-business tool chest. It is helpful for all types of business in all sectors, because the idea is the same – to get people as excited about your business as you are.

Think about it. We are always asked what it is we do. Having a quick, interesting, powerful answer is such an easy, simple sales tool, yet is also one of the most effective. You never know when or where an important lead may appear. A powerful elevator pitch may lead to opportunities that you did not even know existed. You do indeed only have one chance to make a good first impression.

And if you're inspired into insincere action with a 'larger than life' elevator pitch, a word of warning. Mirror neurons in our brain enable us to subconsciously identify lying and dishonesty in others, without even knowing why we know. Your pitch has to be genuinely enthusiastic and honest.

Keeping your pitch fresh

Every business grows and changes, and your pitch needs to grow and change with it. You can have the most creative logo, the slickest strapline, the most beautiful brochures and the most cutting-edge website, but if your elevator pitch is out of date, you're missing one of your most important opportunities to sell.

In other words

The **strapline** is the punchy summary of what your business does, how it does it, or the life you offer your customers.

You know your business better than anyone. How are you keeping abreast of the latest ideas? What continues to set you apart from your competition? How can you speak about your record of quality goods and services and make it relevant to your future plans?

As your audience's needs and expectations change, make sure you change the way you speak about your business. Your language, your approach and what you choose to highlight for a particular audience has got to change over time.

What's in your pitch?

Knowing your business, product, service or issue well is one thing, but how do you convey excitement and spark interest to those outside your organisation? What do you highlight? What do you leave out? And how do those choices change with your audience?

Imagine that you are the guest speaker at a stadium full of business-people, who had to turn up, but don't have to stay. What would you talk about? How would you open? Statistically, about 3 per cent of any audience are actually looking to buy what you sell, and a further 7 per cent might buy if you can match components of your product to bene-fits they are seeking. The rest are varying degrees of 'not interested'.

So, if you get up and start talking about your product's features and benefits, 90 per cent of your audience just left the stadium. Oh dear!

Instead of pitching your product's features, you might make education the focus of your talk. For example, you might title your speech, 'The five biggest threats to your business in the next eighteen months and how to beat them'. With a title like that, the odds are much better that most of the audience will stay around long enough to see whether your content matches your title.

This is an important focus to keep in mind when you're invited to pitch your knowledge and expertise (as opposed to your products) in seminars and demonstrations. By leading with what the audience is likely to find of interest and linking that to what you do, you are more likely to capture the attention of your prospective customer.

The qualities of a great pitch

There are a few things to consider in order to create a fabulous elevator pitch:

→ Look back at the unique selling point (USP) you created in Chapter Three. What is the problem your business solves? Every successful business eases a pain or provides a pleasure for someone.

→ Is it simple and easy to understand? Use plain English, be interesting, keep it clear and have conviction.

→ Would people want to know more? The idea is to entice them to want to delve deeper into what you do. Instead of saying, for instance, 'I am a beautician,' you might start with, 'I help people feel more ready to face the world.'

→ Does it accelerate your heart rate? A great pitch is a passionate pitch.

In this type of 'selling' your goal is to build rapport and credibility with your audience through the value of the content you share with them.

Next: stop talking, start listening

The first thing we do when we phone customers or see them in person is to ask them an opening question. The answer to that tells us right from the outset whether or not they're in the market for our product. And it's all right if they're not. The purpose of a pitch is to further qualify the prospect and to discover the real reasons why they might need our offer.

Within the armoury of important sales skills, it's vital not to overlook the power of listening. Here are five ways to be an effective listener:

→ Face the prospect and listen attentively without interruption.

→ Pause before replying, and restate any points the prospect has just raised.

→ Ask gentle, humorous or probing questions for clarification.

→ Relax, stay calm and enjoy the conversation.

→ Use closed questions to help the prospect give firm answers where necessary.

When you are presenting to a prospect, you are usually some way into the sales funnel. You have another opportunity to reinforce their belief and confidence in you, but you don't need to tell them everything, otherwise they may take your advice but not your services. As US sales guru David Sandler colourfully says, 'Don't spill your candy in the lobby.' Don't give it away the minute you walk through the door.

There is a fine balance between offering enough information for your prospect to make the right decision and giving away free consultancy. You will know the balance, but be very clear not to overstep it in your own business and give away too much of your knowledge for free.

Begin trial closing questions early in your pitch. Trial closes can include 'Is this what you had in mind?' (kinaesthetic prospect), 'Can you see this working for you?' (visual prospect) and 'Does that sound like something you'd be happy with?' (auditory prospect), and should connect to the communication style the prospect has demonstrated, if possible. There will be more information on this in Chapter Eight.

From pitch to presentation

A planned presentation goes further than a pitch. It is a logical, step-by-step process to discuss again what your product offers and how it will benefit the prospect. The planned presentation is infinitely more powerful than the random presentation, not least because the prospect feels that there is some order to the conversation and that everything will be addressed. Here are the top ten ways to create a good planned presentation:

1 *Start with your objective.* Know what you want to say, why you want to say it and what you want the audience to do or think afterwards.

2 *Know and understand your audience.* What is their level of knowledge? What information needs do they have? How attuned are they to different forms of delivery?

3 *Script, review, rewrite, rehearse.* Ask a colleague (ideally one with little technical or industry knowledge) to criticise and then rewrite until you are happy and confident with the content.

4 *Structure.* Remember this sequence: signpost, say and summarise. In simple terms, tell them what you're going to tell them, then tell them, then tell them what you've told them. Repeat key points three times in this way. This technique was most famously and memorably used by Martin Luther King in his magical 'I have a dream...' speech.

5 *Keep it short and simple.* Stick to just five key messages and keep the talk to no more than 20 minutes – any longer and the audience will go to sleep. Use language that is appropriate to the audience. This generally means avoiding all jargon.

6 *Choose the appropriate style.* This will depend on the numbers and the venue. A team briefing in the office can be fairly informal, but still needs to give information, have a structure and have an outcome. A theatre-style presentation, on the other hand, needs to be more formal with more in-depth preparation and attention to achieving professional delivery.

7 *Engage the audience.* Eye contact, body language and hand gestures all build rapport. Check at rehearsal that you are not overdoing any gestures. You could also involve the audience, where relevant, by asking them to participate or simply asking for a show of hands in response to a question or two.

8 *Use appropriate audiovisual equipment.* Flipcharts and overhead projectors, PowerPoint or similar software – there are so many routes to present your message. Good graphics (large and simple), colour, movement and sound add drama and interest, but don't let them take over the presentation.

9 *Provide meaningful handouts.* Copies of your speech, prompt cards or screen shots are the minimum you should provide. Remember, writing is a different medium and style and presentation should reflect this, allowing you to develop your case further.

10 *Finish with a summary and call to action.* Always close with a brief summary of what you have said, followed by a call to action or a question.

Pitching by degrees

Have you ever heard the saying, 'It's not what you know, but who you know that counts'? Today, although what you know is much more important than ever, it is still true that contacts matter. Sadly, far too many people leave this process entirely to chance.

The first rule of networking is to tell everybody what you do. This is because people like to deal with people who they either know first hand or have been recommended to them.

A very famous piece of research by Hungarian Frigyes Karinthy suggested that everyone in the world is connected to everyone else by a chain of only five people. This is the theory of 'six degrees of separation'. It's one of the reasons why networking is so powerful. It's not just the people who you meet as you network. It's all the people that they know, with whom they can potentially connect you.

Imagine that you are in the centre of a 'web' of friendships, relationships and contacts. You then get to know someone new who, of course, has their own relationship web. The result is that the two webs are linked by a new thread. If you've ever used any of the online networking systems, such as LinkedIn, 4Networking and Ecademy, you'll know what I mean.

When you step back, you can see that there are millions of webs, each interconnected with each other. And the key to networking is to join those webs that are populated by members of your target market and other people they buy from.

If you've never tried networking, go along to a number of events and start talking to people. The ritual, of course, is to ask what business the other person is in and exchange business cards. But there are plenty of fresh and exciting variations that take the pressure off, such as by allowing you to present informally to the room for 60 seconds, or even to get a copy of the attendee list for future correspondence.

How will these contacts help your business? Well, neither of us know yet, do we? But, successful people do tend to be helpful people. One of the reasons for this is that many people have helped them to get where they are today. They tend to be happy to give information, advice and, eventually, introductions.

Tips for networking

Ready to start networking and promoting your business? Here are some tips to get yourself mentally prepared for 'working a room':

→ Boost your confidence and feel your best – give yourself a pep talk and a mental (or physical) round of applause to get you in a positive and dynamic frame of mind.

→ Be early – people will then have to come to you when they enter the venue or room.

→ Look out for the body language and know which groups to join. Open groups, where shoulders and lower legs are pointing outwards from other group members, suggest the conversation is relaxed and open to others to join.

→ Get your conversation openers ready – read the papers, but also know about the industry or lifestyle of the people who'll be there.

→ Have your 30-second commercial ready and waiting – don't miss the opportunity to tell people clearly what you do.

→ Ask questions – people will often tell you much more than they mean to if you're really listening.

→ Take business cards with permission to follow up – and always follow up.

→ Don't get too drunk or be too controversial. You want to be memorable, not infamous.

→ Be an ally to the person alone by rescuing them and starting a conversation.

→ Never leave someone without a host – introduce them to other people and groups before you move on.

→ If you are there with colleagues, ensure you have a plan of who you want to meet or the targets you have set for yourself.

→ Don't slip into your comfort zone – suggest to colleagues that you both take a different side of the room and meet at the far-side, rather than simply chatting to each other all evening.

→ Attend different types of networking groups and events to decide which ones work best for you.

→ Make notes on business cards for any specific opportunities you have identified.

→ Ask other people to introduce you if there are particular guests you want to speak to. Use the principle of six degrees to your advantage.

→ Always make a note afterwards of who you met, who you must follow up with and what additional action you will take. And do it. Make it part of your whole sales plan.

And here are some tips to keep in mind for those gleaming opportunities to pitch your business:

1 *Begin with the end in mind*. What are you looking to gain? Most often the pitch is used as a tool to capture enough interest to warrant a formal presentation.

2 *Sell, sell, sell*. What are you really selling? You are selling yourself! You're selling your dream. Look back to Chapter Three – be confident and show your passion.

3 *Keep it simple*. You should deliver a clear, compelling and simple image of your opportunity that is easy to remember and repeat. You want the audience to say, 'I get it!'

4 *Image is everything*. The pitch must implant a clear image of your opportunity in the mind of the audience.

5 *Adapt your presentation to the audience*. The pitch you use for an investor might not be the same as that for a supplier or a journalist.

6 *Lay out the benefits*. Demonstrate how your business will impact consumers and showcase the return to the investors.

7 *Differentiate yourself from the competition*. Focus on outlining the special features of your product/service that give you the edge over the competition. Time permitting, summarise the competitors and insert facts or statistics where necessary.

8 *Don't forget the numbers*. Depending on the audience, you need to insert a snapshot of your financials and other critical data.

9 *Be memorable*. Use your creativity and imagination. Put a tag on it! For example, Tesco says 'every little helps', whilst Xbox encourages you to 'jump in'. Tangerine Trees, if you're interested, emphasises our 'refreshingly straightforward thinking'.

10 *Conclude with a call to action*. For example, 'Thank you for the opportunity to pitch my idea. I'd be happy to provide greater detail over a lunch.' The best pitch is useless without any follow-up action.

11 *Practise, practise, practise!* While there are always a few naturally gifted speakers out there, the more you rehearse your pitch the more

naturally it will flow and the more confident you will appear. Remember that showing confidence and passion helps sell your idea.

12 *Don't give up.* Some people may not understand your opportunity at first, so don't get discouraged or quit. We've all heard the infamous (and deeply reassuring) stories, like that of Decca Records, the record label that turned down the Beatles.

Web bonus

At our website, **www.forentrepreneursbooks.com**, click on the 'Selling for Entrepreneurs' button. On the link for Chapter Five you'll find tips on body language and conversation openers that will give you a head start in networking.

Key points

→ It's strangely common to encounter business owners and entrepreneurs who struggle to say clearly and quickly what their business does.

→ Talking to more people is a very important step in the sales process towards selling more, and the early stages of these conversations should always include a clear 30-second commercial about your business.

→ An elevator pitch, just like a USP, won't last for ever, as expectations, markets and customers change. Make sure your pitch evolves, too.

→ A stadium pitch goes one step further to addressing a big audience, rather than a one-to-one conversation.

→ Be careful that your pitch doesn't give away all your best advice, or you might not be invited back to a sales appointment.

→ Everyone in the world, so the theory goes, is connected to everyone else by five other people. This 'big picture' thinking could be very useful to your sales.

→ Plan your sales pitch presentations to make sure you cover all the points your prospect wants to hear.

Next steps

What action will you take to apply the information in this chapter? By when will you do it?

_____

_____

_____

_____

Overcoming objections

Chapter Six

Objections are great! A prospect with genuine objections (as opposed to one with no actual need or interest in your product) is emotionally committed to the outcome of the conversation.

The three most common objections, ones you may be all too familiar with, are:

→ 'It's too expensive.'

→ 'I don't have time.'

→ 'I need to think about it.'

We'll examine all of these – and more – in the course of this chapter.

Why won't they buy?

Objections that are overcome move the prospect from one stage of the funnel to the next. This is one stage of traditional sales that does briefly link back to the thought process of the prospect, although sadly, in my experience, often in an attempt to belittle their views rather than help answer their questions.

However, this is one of the first opportunities into really entrepreneurial sales strategies. Very often, businesses will try to overcome objections as and when they arise, without proactively considering things from a prospect's point of view. Maybe prospects don't see the value, don't really understand the offer, think it's too good to be true, want a way to find out more without committing to a conversation or just don't have enough faith in you.

Have you ever wondered how many people nearly bought from you, but weren't quite convinced? Sometimes you'll know because they told you they were going elsewhere, or they stopped communicating with you. And sometimes you may never know that they were seriously considering you.

Scientific focus and measurement of activity within your sales funnel helps to answer the question of why someone doesn't buy. At each stage of your sales process you will see the prospects who chose not to move on to the next stage. This is a goldmine of information for your business, because collating the reasons 'why not' will give you an invaluable insight into objections getting in the way of your business success.

What are they really saying?

It's extremely important to ensure you never answer unasked questions. This is one of the booby traps for all salespeople. Maybe you've been in this situation yourself where an otherwise enthusiastic prospect says, 'It's too expensive.' Did you respond with a whole host of extras, an instalment plan payment scheme or a special offer reduced price? That's logical, but not if it is done without understanding the context of the prospect's comment. They didn't ask what else could be thrown in or what payment plans you offer. So first we must understand more about their comment.

Did they mean it's more expensive than what's offered by a competitor? Or is it just more expensive than they expected, in which case, you want to find out the basis for their original expectation. Or is it too expensive until they get paid on Friday? You can no doubt see examples of how this could apply in your business's world.

If someone doesn't buy from you based on your matching of your benefits to their needs in the questioning stage, it means they have objections. Don't confuse this with 'not interested'.

If they get up and walk away (or put the phone down) with no more questions, no 'I'll think about' and no reasons why they won't buy from you, then they're not interested. And there is no point chasing those people down the street. Someone or something else might meet their needs better.' They are the 90 per cent who are at some level of 'not interested', and if they want to pick up the conversation, they'll do it when they're ready.

If they say, 'Well, it's a bit too expensive' or 'I need to think about it', then this means they just haven't seen the value in your offer yet.

Your ability to handle objections could be the key differentiator in your business. By handling objections you are focusing on the prospect, on their needs and their budget, and on the benefits you can bring to them. Consider what some of the main objections could be for your particular business and try to script some answers that would overcome them.

The main objections

As outlined at the start of this chapter, the three main areas where objections occur are money, time and belief, so let's address each one in turn.

'It's too expensive'

This objection means that the buyer does not completely understand the value your products bring to the table. Your response should be, 'Would you mind helping me understand how you compare your current provider? Then I might be able to help you see the value in our products/services that your current provider is not able to give you.' And, as you already know your competitors, you'll have a good idea what additional value you really can offer.

In any case, since when has not having enough money ever stopped us from getting something we really want? We find a way to get it. Your answer to this objection is to re-establish the value and remind them of the benefits. Restate the risk reversal offers you are making and the guarantees that come with your product or service. And, if appropriate, split the payments into instalments. Could it be delivered earlier so they can benefit from the cost savings provided more quickly? Is there a price deal due to start soon? Is there another important component or ingredient that you could add to the deal for them?

In other words

Risk reversal is taking the risk involved in every buying decision (wasted time or money, unsuitable product, etc.) and making it a seller's risk instead, through free trials, money back commitments or other techniques.

'I haven't got time to look at this'

This response suggests that you probably offer something that they really need. The chances are that your offering saves time, reduces stress, provides long-term benefits or reliability, am I right? So these people are looking for a low-risk way to learn about or experience your offering away from you. Are there other partnerships you could forge or related products you could sell that would save them time searching elsewhere? Could you offer extra support or an installation period to relieve them of those time pressures?

'I'll think about it'

These people don't believe what you're saying or they don't believe it will work for them. Through testimonials, remind them that other people got great results after initially doubting you and, through risk reversals, make it clear that if it really doesn't work for them they'll be better off anyway.

Don't jump in with a price reduction. Not only will the prospect begin to see that your original price wasn't really based on fact, but they'll expect discounts every time. If you need to offer a concession to seal the deal or get a specific time commitment, make it reciprocal, so that 'if you can do this, I can do that'. For example, 'If you can pick it up, I can add this in', or 'If you can sign today, I can give you this month's price.' You can also add in an extra to the value you would have discounted, perhaps 10 per cent of the original sale price.

But, again, don't just give it away. Always be aware of the impact of price reductions. Not only do they look tatty and contradictory to the image you have created of a successful, powerful, customer-centred, market-leading business, but a 10 per cent price reduction could actually be the equivalent of a 50 per cent profit reduction. You could be increasing, not decreasing, prices. Head back to Chapter Two for a refresher on price increases.

Now let's consider some other common objections.

'No, I'm not interested'

When you hear this common objection, the best response is, 'Thanks for your honesty. Can I ask what your requirements/priorities/expectations are in (this area)?' Keep the customer engaged so that you can learn whether the 'no' is actually 'no' or just 'I have reservations'.

'I am happy with my current provider, thank you'

This is the buyer's polite way of saying 'I'm not interested'. Your response, however, should be different: 'When you say you are happy with your current provider, may I ask what they are doing that you really like/makes your life easier/helps your company save money?' This response will show the customer that you are interested in helping them solve a problem or meet a need. It will also give you an insight into the criteria that prospects respect in your competitors.

'Call me in six months. Then I'll be ready to have this discussion'

While this seems like a 'maybe', and you may be tempted to reschedule a call in six months, take a moment to double check. The best response to this objection is, 'Will six months make a difference in your ultimate decision? If not, can you help me understand what elements need to be in place for us to have this discussion today as opposed to six months from now?' This will again keep the customer engaged in your sales process and force them to continue considering your products.

'I've already spent my budget in this area'

This objection may be a little more difficult to overcome, but it can be done. This is because in most cases, the companies you are working with save back budget for last-minute expenses at the end of the year. Ask the prospect specifically about their budget: 'In order to see if I can potentially help you save money using our products/services, I would love to learn more about how you allocate your budget. Can you spend a few minutes helping me understand your budget process and how much of your budget goes to (this area)?' The more you can learn about their budget, the easier it will be to overcome this specific objection, or plan for it in the future.

What not to do

Here are some things not to do when overcoming sales objections:

→ *Never argue*. Ever. Even if you're right, perception is everything, and you'll probably lose the sale.

→ *Never, and I mean never, attack the person*. Separate the person from the objection and deal with it in its own right. If you fight a person's feelings, more negative emotions will emerge and they'll end up disliking you (which is obviously not a great rapport-building tactic).

→ *Never assume you understand an unspecified emotion or feature*. When overcoming sales objections, don't start answering until you first understand their meaning. 'Too expensive', 'too bulky', 'too slow' – be sure you know exactly what this means in your prospect's world before you jump in with an answer.

→ *Never insult the prospect's opinion*. A comment like 'Your prices are too high' wouldn't be resolved with a response from you like 'Aren't you interested in quality?'

→ *Never avoid the issue*. Don't change the subject or talk in theory, because you're dealing with an emotion here. The prospect is obviously angry or frustrated when they use a word like 'useless' or 'unreliable'. You need to help them vent their emotion.

→ *Don't shift responsibility*. When there is a problem, don't try to blame it on your staff or your delivery people. Your customer will only understand that you are dodging the blame. What your customer wants is for someone to accept responsibility and fix the problem. We all make mistakes. It's what we do to resolve them that matters. A fantastic solution to a problem could actually give you the most loyal customer your business has ever had.

→ *Never make the person wrong*. Perception is reality, so what they believe to be true is true for them.

→ *Never contradict the prospect*. Acknowledge the prospect's perception of a problem. Remember, first meet them where they are and then move them to where you want them to be.

→ *Don't dwell too long on an objection*. If you spend too much time on an objection, you will amplify its importance in the mind of your customer. Better to answer briefly. Your answer should be just long enough to satisfy the prospect, and no longer.

→ *Never guess*. Say, 'I'm sorry, I don't have the answer to that question, but I promise to get the information to you.' When you actually get back to them with a reply, this will show you have the courage to admit what you don't know and that you follow through on your commitments. This can only improve the client's perception of you.

Remember that to have any chance of overcoming sales objections you must first have established mutual trust and confidence. And you must let the prospect know that you are there to be both an advocate and a consultant.

What to do

We've looked at how *not* to deal with objections, so how do you do it? Let's imagine you're now facing a prospect with need, money and interest. But they've raised some objections. There are seven golden rules for overcoming objections like a pro. We'll look at them step by step.

Step 1: Hear the person out and listen fully!

Don't interrupt. Listen patiently and intently. Interrupting a prospect will intensify the objection and cause prospects to become preoccupied with it.

You must completely focus on the prospect to determine the real significance of this objection. Let your genuine concern and sincere interest show on your face. Don't anticipate what the prospect is saying and finish the sentence for them. Just because you've heard every objection under the sun doesn't mean that you needn't listen fully to your prospect's objection. Their perception is unique to them.

If appropriate, close your order book to take the pressure off the prospect. Avoid leaping on the objection before the person finishes.

Step 2: Feed the objection back for confirmation

By restating the objection, you show your concern for the prospect and get clarification in case you misunderstood their point. A prospect might even withdraw their objections once they hear them spoken aloud.

If you listen completely you'll also hear things that are not verbalised. And when you feed back, attempt to use the exact words or phrases that the prospect used.

Step 3: Qualify it as the true objection

When overcoming sales objections you need to qualify it as a true objection. You could say, 'You mean that's the only reason you're not buying?' The answer to this is either yes or no. If it's a fake objection, the prospect will say no, and then you can ask what their other concerns are. But, if the prospect says 'Yes, that's the only reason why I'm not buying', you now know it's the real objection and you can start to answer it.

Step 4: Gently question and explore the objection

Once you have discovered the real objection, invite the person to elaborate fully and ask questions to specify their objection. Frequently, it will take three to seven questions to truly explore the obstacle you face.

Don't accept the superficial reasons offered first, because addressing these won't move you any further forward. These are sometimes called surface problems, and are often just the first thing that sprang into their mind rather than their genuine concern.

Explain the objection, as you understand it, for clarity, and then rephrase your question in a way that incorporates the solution: 'So, if I were able to get you a longer warranty, would that be enough for you to make a decision?'

Step 5: Answer the objection

Having completed steps 1–4 you are in a good position to overcome sales objections. Passion and belief in your products and services has brought you this far, and you must truly believe that the prospect will benefit from what you offer in all the ways you stated. Be confident. Be passionate.

Step 6: Check and test for satisfaction that the objection has been dealt with

As you're overcoming sales objections you need to confirm the answer has been received and understood. Don't reply to the objection and leave it hanging in the air.

If the client says yes, you can lead to a close. If the prospect doesn't feel that their objection has been dispelled, you have some choices.

This is the time to demonstrate value, list comparisons and prove benefits. No one can predict the future but history often repeats itself, so statistics and facts are valuable tools for changing minds. Bring them along. The proof you show is limited only by your imagination and the ability to back it up. When you believe it, they'll believe it.

Step 7: Reorient the person to their criteria of values and lead into a close

It's easy to let an objection disorient and confuse. Use questions that invite the person to clarify what's really important – namely, the major benefits of the product and what is important to their specific situation. These should make the objection look small.

Now that you have uncovered the prospect's needs and reinforced the value of your offering you can bridge to a close. It's often good to describe similar situations when you close. People like to know about others in the same situation as themselves.

Are you managing objections well?

No matter how you sell, you'll face objections. How you handle them will determine whether you make the sale or not. Collectively, how you deal with objections will determine whether you'll stay afloat in the world of sales.

Do you want to improve, but aren't sure where to get started? Think about the last ten sales you lost. A little depressing, perhaps, but a very important and cathartic experience nonetheless. Write down all the reasons you heard from the prospect for not buying your product. Then write a good answer to each, and whenever you have a spare minute, run through them a few times to get to the most natural-sounding answer to the most common objections.

A key area when fact-finding is to establish your clients' budget and show them the value of your products and services in terms of benefits and uniqueness. There's no point wasting your time or theirs if they have a budget of £100 and your product is £1,000. If that is the case, move on and find a new customer. Not everyone is qualified to be your customer.

Remember, price is almost never the issue. Cost or their budget may be, but if you can show your prospects how your products or services will add value, solve the issues they expressed or make their lives easier, you can stop worrying about price.

Work on your listening skills

Although most of us probably think we can listen well, 90 per cent of people have weak listening skills. Even those who know how to listen don't do it all of the time. Think about it. When you are in a conversation and someone is saying something, to be able to understand it you are constantly translating their words into your own experiences and your own words. It's the way our brains are wired. You make sense of other people's words by translating them into what you think they mean.

How many times have you been in a conversation and, before the other person has finished, you are thinking, 'I know what they mean here, I can sort this out'? And the first thing out of your mouth is, 'I know what you mean exactly. It's just like when I ...' But when someone says that to us, it makes our story or our opinion feel insignificant.

Ten levels of listening

Below are listed ten levels of listening. Think about where you are on the scale. Your level will probably vary depending on time, circumstances and your mood. Note your level and concentrate on moving up the levels. The benefits won't just be in your business life. At which of these levels are you, typically, when you are selling?

1 Not there physically. (You didn't hear the conversation or the comment first hand, and this could completely distort your interpretation.)

2 There physically, but not mentally. (Not paying attention at all.)

3 Hearing the speaker but doing something else at the same time (such as looking elsewhere, reading, thinking about a different matter.)

4 Interrupting the speaker early and frequently.

5 Interrupting the speaker later and less often.

6 Allowing the speaker to finish, whilst furiously composing a counter-argument or response in your head.

7 Allowing the speaker to finish, while earnestly trying to understand what is being said, and then replying immediately.

8 Allowing the speaker to finish, pausing, thoughtfully considering what has been said, and then replying.

9 Allowing the speaker to finish, pausing, summarising what you think you heard, and only then replying.

10 Allowing the speaker to finish, summarising what you've heard, and then honing in on limiting beliefs, unhelpful assumptions and generalisations, and unhelpful connections, whilst replying completely.

When you hear ...

Rather than risk anything below level ten for your clients, the following are some answers to common objections that you can keep up your sleeve. Note that each example moves up the listening scale.

The prospect says:	You answer:
'We have no budget...' 'We have no need...' 'We use another supplier...' 'We have a preferred suppliers' list...' 'It's nearly the end of the financial year...' 'It's not my decision...' 'I need to speak to someone else...'	'That's fine. The reason for my call is to...' Or, if you must say more, 'That's fine. I wouldn't expect it to be any other way. The reason for my call is to...' And have a reason!

The prospect says:	You answer:
'We have no need...' 'We have no budget...' 'It's the end of the financial year...' 'It's not my decision...' 'You need to speak to someone else...'	'I understand. At this point most of my competitors would ask you when you do have a budget and arrange to call you back then. I believe that business is built on relationships and I would like to invest the time in getting to know you now.'

The prospect says:	You answer:
'We have an existing supplier...' 'We use in-house solutions...' 'We farm that out to...' 'We have an internal person in charge of that area...' 'We use your competitors.'	'That makes sense. I wouldn't expect it to be any other way and I hear good things about that company/competitor. Many of my other clients said that before they became aware of how what we do complements what they are already doing. What I'd like to do is see you/ask a couple of questions...'

The prospect says:	You answer:
'I don't think your company would be a good match for us.'	'That's interesting. I'd be very keen to understand more about why you feel that way, as it would really help me. Perhaps I could ask you a couple of questions…?'

The prospect says:	You answer:
'We have existing suppliers...' 'We have a preferred suppliers' list...' 'We do this in-house...' 'We contract this out...' 'This is controlled by another department.'	'Thanks for sharing that with me, it sounds like you know what's important. I'm sure that you had good business reasons for putting that in place. Do you mind me asking, what were they?' (And ask as if you mean to get an answer.)

When you stop trying to overcome objections and just listen, you may hear that there really is a problem around whether your product or service is a fit for them.

Be positive! Overcoming objections can be discouraging. As a successful entrepreneur, it is important to realise that you will face objections from the time you begin the sale to the close. Objections simply mean your prospect needs help to understand the value your company brings them. The more you can uncover their needs and help them understand the value of your products/services, the less unexpected objections you will have to face.

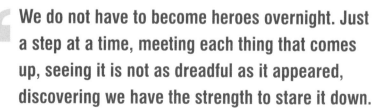

We do not have to become heroes overnight. Just a step at a time, meeting each thing that comes up, seeing it is not as dreadful as it appeared, discovering we have the strength to stare it down.

ELEANOR ROOSEVELT

Selling for Entrepreneurs

Key points

→ Objections normally fill traditional sellers with horror, and the 'school of trained killer salespeople' approach is to dismiss and overcome objections at every opportunity.

→ For the entrepreneur, objections are part of the whole conversation, where buyers want to be convinced, impressed and given an opportunity to test the seller's commitment.

→ There are three common objections – time, money and belief.

→ Not everyone is qualified to be your customer. Sometimes an objection will present reasons why the relationship shouldn't continue.

→ Don't jump in with price reductions to overcome objections.

→ Active listening is the most important skill to handling objections, as you will be able to really hear what is (and is not) being said.

→ Know your competitors, as comparisons could form part of your prospect's objections. Know what they do well and understand how it benefits some customers.

Next steps

What action will you take to apply the information in this chapter? By when will you do it?

_____

_____

_____

_____

Managing your sales

Chapter Seven

Customers have a well-established system for not buying that has served them well for many years. Isn't it time you had one for selling?

Real experts (i.e. entrepreneurs like you) do what works, not necessarily what makes sense at first glance. Prospects and customers work through a series of steps until they feel ready to buy, emotionally and logically. Your job is to help and guide them through this process, whatever it takes.

Zig Ziglar, the fabulously named American sales guru, said, 'Every sale has five potential obstacles; no need; no money; no hurry; no trust; no desire.' And some of these objections, even when overcome completely, make for poor customer relationships. You can only measure what you track and only improve on what you know. By identifying non-opportunities, you don't waste time and energy pursuing them.

You can model your success and replicate the achievements of businesses you admire and aspire to be. And in this chapter, I've made sure to surround you with plenty of quotes and messages from some of those very people.

 ## Everything you want is on the other side of fear.

DAVID SANDLER

Cause and effect

In around 425 BC, the Greek philosopher Socrates put forward what has come to be the foundational law of Western philosophy and Western thought. At a time when everyone believed in the influences of Gods and the elements, Socrates stated simply that we live in a world of law governed by a system of order whether we understand the principles behind it or not.

In what later became known as the 'Socratic method of argument', he used his considerable skills to force people to think through the logical consequences of their thoughts and behaviours. Today we call it the 'law of cause and effect'.

The law of cause and effect says that everything happens for a reason. For every effect or outcome in your life, there is a cause or series of specific, measurable, definable, identifiable causes. This law says that if there is anything you want in life, an effect that you desire, you can find someone else that has achieved the same result or effect, and that by doing the same things that they have done over and over you can eventually enjoy the same results and rewards.

Success, however you define it, is not an accident. It isn't even a result of good luck versus bad luck. External factors are often given great significance in success or failure, but in actual fact they are all part of cause and effect. Even if you haven't taken the time to identify clearly how you got from where you were to where you are today, there has been a series of specific steps that you have taken that have brought you to where you are at this minute. And the fact is, they could have brought you to no other place. It has been your choices and your decisions over the months and years that have inevitably determined the condition of your life and your business at this moment.

The most wonderful part of this is that, at any time, you can start making different choices and different decisions, taking different steps, and you will inevitably arrive at a different place from where you are today. This can be your passport to success in sales as well as in other aspects of your life.

Fall down seven times. Stand up eight.

JAPANESE PROVERB

How the law of cause and effect works

The world is full of millions of people that come from different back-grounds, with every conceivable type of handicap and liability, who have gone on to build wonderful lives for themselves. Often people around them have credited their good fortune to luck. But if you talk to these people and you trace their stories from where they began to where they are now, you will find that luck had nothing to do with their success. And it has nothing to do with yours.

The law of cause and effect cuts both ways. It also says that if there is an effect in your life, such as lack of money, problems in your busi-ness, unsatisfying relationships or any other difficulty, you can trace that effect back to the things that you have done to cause it. And by removing the causes you can begin to remove the effects, sometimes as quickly as overnight.

In its simplest terms, successful, happy, healthy, prosperous people are those that have discovered the laws that govern our lives and have designed their lives so that they are in harmony with those laws. As a result, they experience far more joy and satisfaction, and accomplish far more in a few years than the average person does in a lifetime.

Perhaps the most important corollary to the law of cause and effect is this: 'thoughts are causes' and 'conditions are effects'. Your mind is the most powerful force in your universe. Your thoughts are creative, and they ultimately create your reality. So, if you change your thinking, you change your life.

The key for you to enjoy more of what people call luck is for you to engage in more of the actions that are more likely to bring about the consequences that you desire. At the same time, you must conscientiously decide to avoid those actions that will not bring about the consequences that you desire, or even worse, will bring about consequences that you don't want.

But this philosophy doesn't require radical changes in your current thought process and behaviour pattern. The winning-edge concept says that small differences in ability can achieve huge differences in results. The winning horse in a race isn't 100 per cent faster. It probably isn't even 10 per cent faster. But it still wins the race because it has a small difference in ability, brought about by different training techniques, diet or care. And that's why professional sportspeople practise every single day. Although they know everything there is to know about their sport, they still recognise that their training could cause that 1, 2 or 3 per cent difference between succeeding or not. So, as you make your plans, recognise that they aren't just simply about money or sales or customer numbers, but are also about coaching, motivation, training and time to rehearse your new skills.

Before success comes in any man's life, he's sure to meet with much temporary defeat and, perhaps some failures. When defeat overtakes a man, the easiest and the most logical thing to do is to quit. That's exactly what the majority of men do. NAPOLEON HILL

The power of planning

All well and good, I hear you say, but how does this relate to me and my business?

My reply: planning is the absolute that you must put in place to succeed. The most inspiring and motivational statements about your potential future achievements are no use if you don't plan who you aspire to be, research the causes they have in place, document your introduction of the same causes and measure the results.

This is as true individually as it is in business. As an entrepreneur, you know the dedication that's required in running a company. You also probably know that although 76 per cent of people state that they would like to run their own business, only around 21 per cent ever do. So you're already acting on your plans.

But planning seems like such a dirty word. We associate sales plans with dusty tomes taking up valuable shelf space, or documents bursting at the seams with 'creative' forecasting, produced for the benefit of bank managers or investors. Or with pie-in-the-sky optimism that we might start acting on once all the daily chaos calms down.

Why do we often fail to achieve the results we want when we create plans? Is there a particular format our plan should be in? Is there a level of detail that we must reach before we can succeed? Is there a secret measurement that will force us to stay on track?

Well, quite simply, no.

Extensive research into motivation and achievement shows that the technical differences and processes for goal setting make very little difference to the overall result. How and where you record your goals, what level of detail you go into or even how often you refer back to your plan don't affect the outcome. Now, isn't that refreshing?

The three goal-failure factors

The three factors that do have an impact are known as the three 'I's': insincerity, inconsistency and imprecision.

Insincerity, as the name suggests, means that this is not really a goal we want to achieve. It could be a half-hearted 'wish', a target set by someone else or our response to business or family pressures. New Year's resolutions often fall into this category.

The second 'I' is inconsistency. For example, the renowned psychologist Abraham Maslow said that everything human beings do is based on the underlying balance of strengthening or weakening our self-image. If we are unconvinced of something, we can subconsciously sabotage our chances of succeeding.

And the final 'I' is imprecision. Communication is a slippery concept and the cause of much unhappiness. While you might feel you've communicated the benefits and uniqueness of your product or service perfectly to your prospect, you are stunned when they respond in a way you hadn't anticipated. Did you fail to communicate well? Surely not. Are they being difficult? Possibly. But the most likely explanation is the filters we all use every day have caused them to interpret your request through their own biases, images, experiences and personal factors, such as age and gender. So can you imagine the multiple ways that this communication could be damaged in a sales presentation to a prospect, where neither of you know the other well?

 ## A pessimist sees the difficulty in every opportunity; an optimist sees the opportunity.

WINSTON CHURCHILL

Planning to succeed

Plan well so that you can spend your entire day working. Think of your day as potential minutes, not hours. Use time in the car or travelling to plan, learn new skills and motivate yourself. Here are some effective ways to plan and to succeed:

1 Learn to love selling and commit yourself to becoming outstanding.

2 Decide exactly what you want in life and in business. Decide what you're prepared to pay in order to achieve your goals. Unfortunately there really is no such thing as a free lunch, and nothing worthwhile ever comes without sacrifice.

3 Remember that the key characteristics of successful people are resilience, persistence, flexibility and willpower. Do whatever you need to, to build and sustain these qualities in yourself.

4 Commit to constant improvement and learning.

5 Use your time wisely.

6 Follow the leaders, the best people in business, in sales and in your industry.

7 Guard your integrity. Be true to yourself and your goals.

8 Treat every prospect with kindness and respect.

9 Find out your prospect's judging criteria and agree the process you'll both use to come to a decision.

10 Don't be afraid to ask challenging questions like 'Why did you agree to see me?', 'How many of our competitors are you talking to?' and 'How likely are you to move from your existing supplier?' Done with good rapport and humour, these can be very telling.

What are your goals?

Whose success do you want to replicate? Are you starting to think like the 1 per cent of hugely successful businesspeople? Is anything preventing your business from reaching its potential? It could be personal or business goals that you are looking to achieve, and it is likely to be a combination of the two.

By planning what you want to achieve, documenting every technique and variation you try (and whether it works or not), understanding your competitors and knowing yourself, you are able to replicate success consistently.

By now, you should be feeling that the possibilities for you and your business are only limited by your imagination. This is always a great boost for your passion and enthusiasm.

Get a system to schedule action, not reporting on historical activity but planning the future prospecting schedule and data capture. It doesn't have to be a fancy (or expensive) IT system, just a robust and comprehensive way of planning activity.

Decide on a goal, commit it to paper and then start some action towards it immediately. To do this, break the goal into financial and activity achievements required each and every day. Finding the time and motivation to do this requires huge discipline to keep the pipeline full and create sales. And if you're an entrepreneur your mind may float off to other things. But you won't have a business for long unless you source prospects and create customers.

If you keep your ears and eyes on your customer, you will keep your competitor's foot out of the door. JAMES JONES

Putting your money where your customers are

In terms of sales, your goals will revolve around finding and keeping customers, and this will cost some money as well as your time and energy. How do you decide how much money to allocate to getting and keeping customers? Some sources say 5 per cent of annual turnover. Some say 1 per cent of profit. But these are arbitrary figures based on how well your business is already progressing.

Doesn't it make better sense to find out first of all what a customer is worth to you the first time you sell to them? If you sell to 100 customers, what's their average worth in terms of unit sales and then the corresponding profit? And of those 100 customers, how many will come back if you do nothing else? What is the projected long-term value that each customer will bring to you in net bottom-line profit? Until you know what a customer is and will be worth, you can't possibly understand how much you can afford to spend to acquire them.

When people start a buying relationship, you have an inordinate opportunity to influence them ethically for ever. Customers are coming to you for guidance, and if they favour you with their purchase, it means they trust you. They look to you to have ability, expertise and integrity. If you, at that point, show them the reasons why it's in their self-interest to come back and re-purchase your product or other services or other logical extensions, you will normally get many more customer purchases per year.

The lifetime value of your customer

The strategy that suits businesses of all sizes, margins and sectors is in establishing customer lifetime value. Setting a sales budget can be difficult, but by establishing the customer lifetime value, it is possible to decide how much you are prepared to spend to 'buy' customers. The formula for customer lifetime value is pretty straightforward:

Average cost of initial sale + Average annual spend ÷ Average number of years as a customer

Depending on the type of business you're in and the number of repeat or after-sales purchases, your lifetime value might look like the following.

If a customer spends £6 on an initial purchase, remains a customer for two years and spends £370 per year with you, you might decide that the initial purchase cost is small enough to 'buy' the customer for that first £6, i.e. give them their initial purchase for free (or spend that amount on advertising or otherwise attracting that customer). You would still make £734 over their lifetime, with the opportunity to increase that value through additional sales.

If a customer spends £1,000 on an initial purchase, remains a customer for five years and spends an additional £1,500 per year in after-sales purchases, refills, servicing or whatever is appropriate to your business, you may decide their value is higher as there is more opportunity for upselling, so you could choose to 'buy' that customer for £450, i.e. a free purchase plus additional bonuses and special offers, or a much higher amount spent on advertising and marketing.

Your business might offer a variety of differently priced products and services, so there may be several categories of customer that you need to analyse, as their patterns may be quite different. It might be that your business offers a great 'Trojan horse' product, which gets you through your prospect's door, and then a range of other services behind that, which build loyalty and increase spend. Or your business might have developed a profiling system for recognising likely customer spend – 'if someone buys that product initially, it's usually easy to upgrade them to XYZ'.

By 'buying' customers in this way, you minimise the risk of all your business activity to almost zero. The cost of your sales prospecting and initial offers will simply become part of the cost of acquisition, as you can continue to target customers with offers and opportunities after their initial purchase.

 I have often been afraid, but I would not give in to it. I made myself act as though I was not afraid and gradually my fear disappeared.

THEODORE ROOSEVELT

The characteristics of successful entrepreneurs

This book, and other great sales books like it, will hopefully present you with countless sales techniques that you can use immediately to grow your business and increase your income. But in all successful businesses, there is something deeper driving the entrepreneur's desire to implement such strategies. Let's take a closer look at them.

All highly successful businesses have a driving force that propels their success

At first it seems intangible. You certainly won't read about it in the annual accounts. But it's there, in every single stunningly successful business in the world. These businesspeople are driven by a purpose that goes beyond just making money. Put simply, these are people whose highest purpose is to impact the lives of their customers.

Why does this work so well? It's because if your ultimate drive is to impact other people's lives, you will look at sales in a totally new way. You will be driven, not just by a (totally acceptable, as we discussed in Chapter Two) desire for money and profits, but also by a compelling desire to positively influence the lives of those you come into contact with. It is this mindset that creates stunningly successful businesses. It is this mindset that will create the drive for you to implement everything we are going to cover in the chapters ahead.

Persistence multiplied by perception

For decades, people who run businesses have been told that unrelent-ing determination and a willingness never to give up are key character traits of entrepreneurial success. Technically, this is correct. Persistence and determination are vital. Without them a business entrepreneur will fail. But, and it's a big but, on their own, they can be very dangerous.

The world's most successful entrepreneurs do have incredible deter-mination. But they are very good at deciding what to be determined about. To put it simply, they combine the ability never to give up with the ability to know when something is not working.

This key distinction is what separates the millions who launch new businesses every year from the actual millionaires. If more entrepre-neurs understood it, it could significantly reduce the number of businesses that fail. This is a particularly timely statement if today's gloomy economic news still holds true as you read this.

This teaming of qualities can be summarised as 'persistence times perception'. As long as you're working towards a business goal, you have unrelenting determination and you are perceptive enough to check in with yourself to see if you are working towards the right goal.

Unfortunately, many budding entrepreneurs wake up one day think-ing it would be a great idea to launch a business selling XYZ. They spend about an hour thinking about the decision. Then they spend the next two or five or maybe fifty years trying to make that idea work. And it starts to feel like a job, with all the added negatives of balancing the books and looking after the staff, whilst working for a boss with no plan. It feels like a chore instead of the dream.

That initial decision, of what you are going to sell and what type of business to go into, is the most important business decision you will ever make (and it's never too late to make a new decision!).

How can you be sure you're making the right decision?

→ By ensuring that you are selling a product or service that people want (ideally one they crave) rather than one they just need.

→ By remembering that the only opinion that matters – about benefits, advertising, pricing, distribution and everything else – is that of your customers. What sales techniques they respond to, what they're prepared to pay and what level of service they'll accept – all their decision.

→ By being very clear about what you want to achieve, but never being too proud to be flexible.

Calculate the true value of your customers

You cannot be excellent at sales until you have calculated and utilised the lifetime value of your customers, as we discussed earlier on. Do you know how much a new customer is worth to you over the next year, the next three years, the next ten years?

Drop the concept of 'budgets'. Once you know how much on average each customer is worth, you are in a very powerful position.

A sales budget is self-limiting. Once you break free from that mindset and structure your business so that instead you are allocating funds to 'buy' your new customers, your growth can be extraordinary.

Linked to this is the break-even concept. This says that if you know how much your customers are worth to you over time, it is almost certainly worth you considering breaking even on the initial sale to win that lifetime customer. Do not be deceived by the simplicity of this concept. It has made many people many millions.

In other words

Break-even is where income is exactly equal to expenditure, achieving neither profit nor loss.

Use multiple sales approaches

The typical business only uses one or two sales tools to reach new customers. For your business, your current main sales method may be referrals or your store counter, advertising, the internet, PR or cold calling.

Take any business at random and when you look at how they create a new customer, it's not unusual to see that 80 per cent of these come from just one source.

This can have highly significant consequences:

→ The downside – you can run a very successful business using one or two techniques, but it is dangerous. If that source changes or you face unexpected competition, your whole business could be threatened.

→ The upside – if your business is doing well by using just one or two sales methods, what would happen to it if you were to successfully use five, ten or twenty methods? Those who do this achieve exceptional growth.

Using multiple approaches is one of the absolute keys to growing your business and substantially increasing your profits.

Opportunity is missed by most people because it is dressed in overalls and looks like work.

THOMAS EDISON

Keep up your motivation

Staying on top of all these efforts is easier if you have some reminders of your goals and aspirations. Good inspirational and motivational posters reinforce learning and education, boost morale and support personal development for teams and groups and for you on a personal basis. A poster with a powerful message on the office wall helps set you up for the whole day, and over a period of time can actually help to change your life. Words are extremely powerful things.

Selling can be tough on self-esteem, and funny posters help lift morale and create talking points in businesses, organisations and offices. Posters with famous, positive wise words and sayings are inspirational and motivational for staff and customers and help to lift beliefs, values, expectations and reputations.

Use posters that are appropriate for your audience. Humour helps to bring humanity and fun to offices and to other work and educational situations, although a poster that is funny to you might not be funny to someone else, so use your judgement. You could even type up and print out some of the inspirational quotations from famous entrepreneurs and others in this series of books to help keep you motivated and focused.

Key points

→ Managing your sales is in part about creating clear plans that can be put into action and analysed afterwards.

→ It is also about managing your mind, which, as we discussed earlier, is where sales are made or lost.

→ By choosing different steps in your plans, you can reach different destinations. You can even choose to match the steps of other companies you aspire to emulate.

→ Big changes are rarely necessary to achieve different effects or outcomes. A 1 per cent difference could set you apart sufficiently to achieve your goals.

→ There are three major factors that impact the success of a plan, and they are related to your view of your plan, instead of how you present or use your plan.

→ By 'buying' the initial sale from a customer, you can put your plan into action more quickly, as you build a customer base that you can grow over time.

Next steps

What action will you take to apply the information in this chapter? By when will you do it?

_____

_____

_____

_____

Closing techniques

Chapter Eight

At some point, your selling process has to move from persuasion and information into a phase where you enable the sale to be closed, discarded or postponed for another day. Depending on what you sell and how, that point could be after two minutes or six months. The purpose of closing is to help fulfil needs, solve problems and satisfy desires that were established during your demonstration. It is important that you use your tools of salesmanship to show customers how the product you're showing will meet their needs, solve their problems and fulfil their desires.

In other words

Persuasion is the influencing stage of the sales process, often mapped to the buyer's desire stage. This is where a particular seller attempts to influence the buyer to use their specific offering.

Asking for the close

You should never ask bluntly or rudely for the order or the sale. 'So, do you want it or not?' is likely to have only one outcome. But sometimes people really need their hand held from one stage to the next. Questions like 'How would you like to pay?' or 'Would you like to take it with you now?' are softer and more comfortable for everyone concerned. And if you've addressed any objections before you get to this stage, you know they are still interested in the possibility of buying.

Are you looking back at those questions (or equivalent questions suited to your business) thinking, 'I could never ask that'? Then have a quick look again at Chapter Two and consider your own mindset about the selling process. To hesitate to close a prospect who wants to buy what you sell is only based on your limiting beliefs about sales.

Closing the sale, the fulfilment stage of selling, is the right thing for entrepreneurs to do if your solution is absolutely right for the prospect. Have you covered all the potential objections clearly? Closing should simply be a logical progression of ideas bringing about a decision. In selling, this means the process used to bring your customer to a decision, whether it is a yes or a no.

Closing is the concluding stages of the sales process, where a decision is reached by both parties about how to progress the relationship.

Naturally you must make sure you are speaking with the person who makes the buying decisions. Sometimes a person won't say yes to your product or service because they're not authorised to do so. If this is the case, your questions and active listening should uncover the fact, so find out whether there is anybody else involved in this decision that your prospect recommends you speak with.

The traditional approach

In traditional sales books and training courses, a lot of attention is given to closing and there is often a lengthy section on specific closing techniques. It is implied or even said that if you have 20 or 57 or 102 different ways to close the sale up your sleeve, you can keep on closing until the poor customer gives up the fight and says yes.

This style of selling forms confrontational situations, which create resistance in customers, high stress and ultimately burnt-out salespeople who become unproductive, feel like failures and eventually quit.

There are certainly some highly successful superstars of selling who operate this way, and we can all look at them and say, 'If they can do it, why can't anyone?' In fact, the more observant of you will notice that I promoted just such a technique in Chapter Seven. There are some people whose personality is so strong that they never take no for an answer in any situation and they are usually quite obnoxious people when you get to know them. Most people aren't like that and most people can't sell successfully using that style because they care too much to ride roughshod through conversations.

Yet, as entrepreneurs, we want to replicate successful behaviour to help our businesses succeed, so we perpetuate it in our selling approach. And we end up being frustrated that our sales results just don't measure up.

One of the motivational tools used when sales results take a down-turn is to remind ourselves that 'selling is a numbers game'. Now, that statement is true, but have you really taken a look at the numbers? Some of the ratios are so bad that I can't believe that we actually accept these results and keep pushing ourselves to work this way.

Calvin had a hard-sell approach
to closing the sale.

 Enjoy failure and learn from it. You can never learn from success. JAMES DYSON

The better way

The good news, if you struggle with the stress and low success rates of the traditional closing methods, is that there is a better, less stressful and ultimately more successful way to sell.

This approach is based upon finding people who really want and need your product or service and letting them buy it. What could be easier than allowing someone who desperately wants what you're offering to buy it?

There are two major differences between the traditional approach and the less stressful approach. The traditional heavy closing approach

Selling for Entrepreneurs

is based on the premise that prospects are scarce and if we get the opportunity to talk to anyone we must do everything we can to convince them to buy. The second element is that the traditional approach is all about our need to sell, rather than what our customer wants. Sometimes customers feel like they've been manipulated. If people feel tricked or otherwise betrayed, not only will they not buy from you now, but they may well never buy from you in the future. And they could even tell all their friends about their experience. In particular, beware of using unsubtle techniques with professional buyers, who can usually see them coming from miles away.

The less stressful approach, in contrast, is based on the knowledge that there are lots of potential customers in the market and our effort should be put into finding the ones who are ready and willing to buy our services. If we let enough people know about our service and let them experience what we have to offer in dozens of different ways, when the time is right, they will seek us out.

The second part is that this approach is totally based on the prospect's needs, rather than our own. Our customers trust us because they learn that we are not out to rip them off, which is so much an element of resistance in the traditional sales methods. As you remember, the prospect's fear of making a mistake is one of only two real reasons why selling can be difficult.

Most of your effort should go into developing tools that attract the attention of prospects, because they provide some element of value to the client. By consistently demonstrating value, you will attract enough interest from customers who want your products and are ready to talk to you with minimal resistance.

You can develop effective and efficient sales processes by focusing on what customers want and by finding low stress but high impact ways to let them know that you have what they want. If you do a good job of selling by identifying customer needs and matching your offer to what they want, you don't need dozens of different closing techniques to finalise the sale.

All you need to do is say, 'That seems to be what you want. How would you like to pay for that?' If you have the belief and the passion in yourself, your business and your offering, it will happen for you!

The traditional approach in action

Have you ever wished (even in the darkest recesses of your mind) that you could behave like one of the salespeople who graduated from the school of trained killers? The type who won't take no for an answer, and who pursue every possible angle until the poor prospect gives up, admits defeat and ultimately buys just to get you out of their office? Let's see how it works in action.

I want you to imagine yourself as a decision maker in a large organisation. You agree to meet with a seller who's been trying to set up a meeting with you for several months. When he mentioned the business results his company was achieving with your competitor, you decided it couldn't hurt to learn a bit more.

After a ten-minute discussion, you start to notice that nearly all his sentences end with a question: 'Don't you agree?', 'I'm sure you've experienced that?' or 'Is that true here?' This traditional closing technique is designed to get your head bobbing up and down. The more you say yes, the easier it'll be for him to get your business.

After sharing a bit more about his company's services, he begins to implement another closing technique by asking:

'Do you usually start out with weekly or monthly orders?'

'Can you get this through purchasing fairly easily?'

'Do you agree that this methodology would be helpful?'

By getting you to agree to small things first, he's warming you up for the big close.

Your head is spinning and thoughts are racing through your mind: 'I'm not ready to get started on anything right now. I'm just learning. Besides, I don't know if it's even worth it to make a change. I have thoughts and concerns, but if I voice them, he'll just stay longer.'

But he persists. He's really good at closing. He moves into the next closing technique. With a winning smile on his face, he says to you, 'We can get going on this by mid-month.'

By now you're almost certainly feeling a bit pushed, or maybe even very pushed. You're not ready to make any kind of decision on the spot like this. Trying to get out of this situation politely and get him out of your office, you ask, 'How much money are we talking about?' No matter what he says, it will always be too much!

He comes straight back in with yet another closing approach. He looks at you and says, 'We're really busy right now. So many people are ordering. If you don't go ahead right now, I have no idea how long it will take or even if the pricing will stay the same. I've heard it's going up.'

You tell him you'll have to take your chances, because it's out of the question for you to make decisions so quickly. And you think to yourself that is was presumptuous of him to think you would.

He isn't to be deterred. He launches into another closing technique. Pulling a list of testimonials out of his briefcase, he puts them across the desk in front of you one by one. 'Look at all the great companies who we work with,' he says. 'They love us. We've done great things for them.'

Feeling as if you are running out of options to escape, you glance quickly at your watch and say, 'I'm sorry. I have to run to a meeting right now. Thank you so much for your time.'

'If you act now, we've got this great promotional offer,' he says, using his final winning close approach as you move him out the door. 'We'll throw in twenty hours of free training and a new iPod.' For the first time in this meeting, you feel good – because he's gone.

That's what happens when someone insists on using all their best closing skills. They close and they close. At the same time, they irritate their prospective customers. They might also instil an element of fear in the prospect's mind that opening up this conversation in the future would mean a similarly painful experience.

On the other hand...

Now let's look at what the very best salespeople do. They don't actually employ any special closing techniques at all. They simply focus on understanding their prospect's business and helping them achieve their desired outcomes. Closing, or more realistically a mutual decision to move forward, is achieved because all parties are happy with the opportunity.

Instead of talking about their product or service, smart entrepreneurs ask lots of good quality questions. They keep their focus on their prospect's business challenges and the gaps that need to be closed to achieve their objectives.

If it's relevant to your business, you could also ask them questions in order to get them to say what it would cost them if they didn't buy your product. A disaster without insurance, a car accident because of bald tyres, a poor product launch because of a lack of market research. Cost can be financial, time or reputation, amongst other things, and it can be useful to call this to the customer's attention.

Then, knowing that corporate decisions take a while to make and often involve many people, good salespeople simply suggest the logical next step.

Many entrepreneurs have little or no experience in outside sales. Finding new prospects and explaining features and benefits can be difficult for an entrepreneur who isn't sales-oriented. But inexperience can be crushing when it is time to close the sale, and can result in irritated prospects instead of healthy bank accounts and happy customers.

Tips for success in closing

Although it may be difficult, closing doesn't have to be painful or bewildering. Here are a few basic pointers to help demystify this potentially awkward process.

Close from the beginning

Don't confuse this idea with the hard sell we just saw; the cut-throat approach alienates many potential customers. Instead, explain your agenda. Tell the prospect exactly what you're selling and how it can benefit their business. Being upfront about your intentions promotes an honest, mutually respectful and rewarding discussion, helping you both to view the sale as an opportunity worth considering. Prompt them to ask questions, try to create an open, honest conversation and perhaps even mention some concerns of your own. From the very beginning, all of your talking, thinking and action is directed towards uncovering whether this is right for both parties, and if so, helping them buy.

Spotting the buying signals

Learn to recognise when potential customers are ready to buy. A customer might indicate they're ready by asking questions about the product or the buying process, like 'How long would delivery take?' 'What does that button do?' or 'Is an upgrade available?' Other signs include complaints about previous vendors and interested comments such as 'Really?' or 'Good idea'. They might even make notes on the key points you're making.

Avoid yes or no answers

Don't respond to questions with merely a yes or no, if you can help it. Answer your prospect's queries with questions of your own. Carefully chosen, these return questions can help open the discussion further.

How to use trial closes

People fear making the wrong decision. Because of this fear, people will put off making any decision. It is very important that your prospects make a decision, whether it is a yes or a no, so that they feel in control of the conversation and you can react to that decision and close again or move on if necessary. Not everyone is qualified to be your prospect, and uncovering that before you both make a mistake should be recognised as a real success.

A closing question asks for a final decision. A trial close question is one that asks prospects for an opinion. Trial closes should be non-threatening questions that ask how your prospective customer feels about what you have presented.

It is much easier for the prospect to make decisions on minor points and for you both to judge how the relationship should progress. That is the purpose of the trial close questions. The prospect makes a series of smaller decisions rather than being confronted by one large decision. Trial close questions give you an indication of whether the prospect is interested. But they should be real questions, not the staged ones from our sales rep example earlier.

Each trial close is like a traffic light, with the prospect at the controls. As long as they give you a 'yes' (a green light), you can keep on moving with the presentation and progress towards the sale. The minute you hit a 'no' (a red light) you have to stop, handle the objection and then ask more trial close questions. When a prospect continually responds negatively to trial close questions, shorten your presentation and, if necessary, gracefully finish and move to another appointment.

Remember, not everyone is qualified to be your customer and your product might not be right for them. If your prospect is waiting for a polite opportunity to say no, better to hear it now than after days, weeks or months of effort. Keep the conversation open and sincere to give everyone an opportunity to express their thoughts.

When a customer responds to trial close questions with maybes or indecision, you are not ready to start closing. The prospect isn't convinced of the value of your product.

The importance of attitude: yours and theirs

For every sales presentation you should establish a closing question that is designed to induce action. It is extremely important when asking the close questions to have a completely positive mental attitude. Be confident and passionate about your product, assume your prospect is going to buy and never doubt their intentions to do so. Your confidence and assumptive attitude will affect the customer's confidence and attitude in making a decision.

By the same token, you want to help the prospect remember at all times that your future doesn't rely on whether they buy or not (you never want to make your prospect feel pressured by guilt or responsibility). Don't give the impression that you've made the decision for them.

The purpose of the assumptive close question is to make it easier for the prospect to reach a decision. Direct questions like 'Do you want it?' put a lot of pressure on the person. It makes it more difficult for the prospect to reach a decision.

Closing questions primarily do two things. They help the person who is interested to decide and they make it easier for the person who is not interested in buying to tell you so. Your primary goal is simply to bring your customer to a point of decision. You must help them overcome their natural tendency to procrastinate.

Once you have asked your close question, stop talking and listen. When you ask the close question you must allow the prospect a chance to answer. They will answer with an objection or with a positive response. If it is an objection, handle it and ask a new question – based on the new information, the prospect can now make a 'new' decision.

If a prospect hesitates to answer, then just wait. It may take a minute or two but do not talk. You are actively listening to all the available signals, not just the prospect's words. If there is a pause, then the prospect is merely thinking through what you've said. Allow them time to do so.

Get the closing mindset

Here are some tips on how to get the mindset that will make closing easier:

1 Close with a strong positive mental attitude. Assume that if you identify a good match your prospect is going to buy, and never doubt their intentions to do so.

2 By the same token, you want to relax your prospect by letting them feel it doesn't matter to you financially whether they buy or not. Everyone likes to buy ... nobody likes to be sold.

3 Never pressure your prospect with direct questions like 'Do you want it?'

4 If you really believe it is true, reassure your prospect that they are making the right decision by purchasing.

5 Relax. At this point in the sales process, you can make your customer uncomfortable or relaxed, depending on what your attitude and feelings are. If you relax, they will relax. This helps establish trust and confidence.

6 Don't make your offer too wordy and confusing. A confused, intimidated prospect never buys. Make the close as simple as possible. Go slow.

Mike Southon, co-author of the fantastic *Beermat* series of entrepreneurial guides, offers links to podcasts, blogs and slides on his website, **www.beermat.biz**.

Watch for the signals

Customers give out lots of verbal and non-verbal clues that can tip you off when they are ready to buy, for example:

→ They start to ask lots of questions.

→ They talk about how it would be when they own the product.

→ They smile or hold eye contact.

→ If you are selling to a couple, they become more affectionate (with each other!).

→ They want to see the demonstration again.

→ They use positive body language signals like nodding (without you using your manipulative sales rep's techniques).

→ They lean forward in their chair.

→ They unfold their arms or uncross their legs.

→ They stop thinking positively (with their head to one side) and bring their head down to look you in the eye.

→ They say, 'Will you go over that one more time?'

This is not a complete list of buying signals and you have probably noticed others in your work. Watch for them and you will get better at knowing exactly when to close.

Key points

→ Traditionally, closing has been taught as the stage where the prospect's defences are down, so all that is left for the sales-person is to beat the prospect into submission with fake questions.

→ It is very important to note that many prospects would not progress to taking an action unless the salesperson guided them through it, so entrepreneurial closing is a vital part of the sales process.

→ Today's entrepreneurial salesperson doesn't use tricks or attempt to cause the prospect to surrender. The only successful buying scenario is one where both parties win.

→ Asking lots of genuine questions and keeping the conversation open and honest is the most effective way to close. Entrepreneurial sellers may even raise their own concerns about the future relationship.

→ Questions give the prospect opportunities to decide whether they are really interested, or to tell you if they aren't.

→ Identifying the buying signals relevant to your specific sectors and products will help you to know when a prospect needs more reassurance and when they are ready to sign.

Next steps

What action will you take to apply the information in this chapter? By when will you do it?

_____

_____

_____

_____

Indirect selling

Chapter Nine

Now let's consider some ways of selling that don't involve face-to-face meetings. Every stage of the sales funnel process will have written or non-spoken information that continues to sell when you're not there. It must reinforce benefits, overcome objections and answer questions. It could include advertising, websites, corporate literature, sales presentations, sales contracts, product information, invitations and so on. What makes for a great indirect sales tool? When you're first creating advertising for your small business, it's very tempting to go for the flashiest, cleverest, artiest adverts. But adverts with impact are those that actually generate customers.

Two types of advertising

Brand advertising tells you how great the company is and how old and established they are, or it gives a quick reminder of their product which you already know very well and don't have to think too hard about. Great if you're Coca-Cola or BMW, not so good if you don't have those kinds of budgets.

Direct response advertising is designed to create an immediate response or action – a visit, a call, a click. It tells a complete story, with factual, specific reasons why your offering is superior at meeting the needs of your audience. It is salesmanship in print. It overcomes sales objections, it answers all major questions, it promises performance or results, and it backs those promises with warranties or guarantees. This is the only advertising your money should go anywhere near. For much of this chapter we're going to be looking at online advertising – either through your company website or other adverts – but many of the principles apply to all indirect selling media, as you'll discover.

Pay per click

If you've never tried the revolution in direct response advertising that is pay per click, this is something you really need to master. Pay per click, as the name suggests, is an advertising system that only charges you when someone clicks on a link to your website.

These online adverts appear in the results from search engines like Google. So, for example, if you typed 'hotels in Cornwall' into the search box, you'd get pages and pages of results that match your search. These are called 'natural' or 'organic' results, and they are found by the sophisticated technology of the search engine. It's the engine that decides in what order the results come up.

Alongside those natural search results, at the top and to the right of the first few search results pages, you'll find paid results. The beauty of these adverts for the entrepreneur is that you appear there for free. You pay only when someone actually clicks on your advert to visit your website, for an agreed-upon small amount per click. You can set a daily limit that you are willing to pay, so you never need to spend more than you plan and you can start as small as you like. If, for example, you are paying 20 pence per click, and you have set a limit of £20 per day, once your advert has yielded 100 clicks, it disappears for that day. On which page and where on that page your ad appears depends partly on how much you are willing to pay per click, compared to your competitors. Naturally, popular search terms like 'dieting' cost more than more specific or obscure terms.

Of course, the real test of the effectiveness of such ads is the conversion rate. That is, the number of people who actually buy something when they come to your website. Having thousands of clicks (for which you are paying) means nothing if they don't result in sales.

Pay per click is the perfect online demonstration of testing and measuring your marketing. You can measure your advert's click-rate and conversion rate and constantly try to improve your advert copy to increase them. You can also include negative keywords so your advert doesn't show against irrelevant search entries. Visit Google and type in 'Adwords' to the search engine to learn more about how the system works.

How does your website rank?

The 'importance' of your website is a key part of where it appears in the 'natural' search results on search engines, but it also plays a big part in where your pay-per-click advert appears, regardless of the amount you bid. To check your current Google ranking score, download the Google Toolbar from the Google search page, which includes a Page Rank gauge. One you have installed the Toolbar application, every website you visit will show a page ranking. Visit a popular website like **www.bbc.co.uk** to see a really high page ranking in action.

You should be aiming for a page rank of over three for your own website. And the best way to do this is to increase your 'importance' by adding incoming-only links.

Links to your website could come from happy customers, industry organisations, partner businesses, news sites, article and opinion sites, and others who are highlighting your advice for their own site visitors. Reciprocal links are disregarded by the search engines, so incoming-only (when they link to you, but you don't link back) and three-way links (when you and two partner businesses decide to create a triangular link, with each of you linking to one of the others) will increase your ranking. Visit **www.alltheweb.com** to see who currently links to you.

Registering your details in online directories or posting classified ads is also a good way to improve your search engine importance. But make sure they are good quality sites (with a page rank score over three), otherwise they won't boost your website's score.

Getting people to your site is vital, and for that you need compelling sales copy.

The power of good sales copy

Writing good copy is the single biggest challenge for most business professionals. The words you use act as salesmanship in print and are all that stand between your products and services and a sale. But once you know the basics, writing effective copy is much easier than you think.

Changing the words and phrases that your business uses is the lowest of low-cost exercises you can do, and it will often yield the highest impact. Yet businesses seem to correlate expense and impact so much that when information like this arises, they just don't take the time to act on it.

You can put yourself into the top 5 per cent of businesses in the country with this one simple step in all your sales material.

Writing compelling copy can become the distinguishing feature of your business. Writing compelling copy can initiate sales, causing customers to buy just from your words.

Although copywriting is a daunting term and a concept that most business entrepreneurs shy away from, I want to reassure you right now – copywriters aren't born, they develop. And writing great copy that your prospects and customers can't resist is fully achievable. Writing is a learned skill; it isn't something you have to be born with. Now I'm not suggesting for a minute that writing some great adverts and brochures that make you wealthier would suddenly be a reason to quit the day job and aspire to be the next J.K. Rowling. But perhaps you'll discover an untapped skill.

See how you're doing

I encourage you to collect a sample of your literature together – your brochure, price list, telephone script, latest advert, sales proposal, seminar programme, recruitment ads, even a print-off of some pages on your website – and highlight any copy that refers to you without any obvious (stated!) benefit to your audience.

> **I believe in businesses where you engage in creative thinking, and where you form some of your deepest relationships. If it isn't about the production of the human spirit, we are in big trouble.** ANITA RODDICK

Write in chunks

No one knows your business and your customers better than you, so you should certainly try to perfect your copywriting skills before you look for external help.

Focus on having a single conversation with one person over a cup of coffee, and you instantly feel more at ease and will write better copy.

The first thing to remember, a great relief for anyone panicking at the idea of condensing their visionary business into words, is – don't write essays, write bullet points. Bullet points by their nature are simple, concise and easy to write and read. And they're great when you're stuck.

Help the reader get your message by breaking it into bite-size chunks that are easily understood. But one or two words isn't a bullet point, it's a memory jogger, so try to use a full sentence or two.

Use a game

People tend to struggle more with the idea than the actual activity. If this sounds like you, you should try the five-minute writing game.

In the five-minute writing game, you need to write fast and stay on point, so you should do three things:

→ Whatever your subject is, turn it into a question that you will answer in writing.

→ Before you begin to answer the question, write down three keywords that demonstrate the point you want to make or the idea you want to convey.

→ When you start writing, begin with one of your three keywords and include both of the other words in your first paragraph.

Once you have the question and three keywords, type or write as fast as you possibly can for five minutes without backspacing, correcting spelling, thinking about what you write and so on. Just blast it out and try to write as fast as you think. If you do that for five minutes, you'll probably have answered the question and created some of the best copy you've ever written.

Talk it out

If fast typing or writing doesn't seem to do the trick, try recording a conversation. Not just any conversation, but one where you are telling someone else the same things you want to say in your copy. Then play it back and transcribe the bits that sound good. That should certainly give you a great skeleton to build on.

Mind your mind

If fast writing or recording and transcribing don't feel right, maybe it's your mindset that needs attention. Try changing how you feel. Put on some great music, take some exercise or get a change of scenery, or try reading some inspirational words.

Make your message very personal. What do you really want to say? Why is it really so important to you that your readers benefit from your words? Say it like you would to a friend.

Long or short?

As a broad principle, you should write longer rather than shorter copy. As an even broader principle, there will be two groups of people who receive your messages. The first group will have no need or desire for the products and services you sell, so they probably won't even read beyond a powerful headline anyway. The second group will have an active or passive interest in your offering. Long copy, separated with subheadings and plenty of bullet points, will appeal to both types.

Don't take my word for it, test it! See how your market responds to detailed information about your products and services, in print or online.

Testimonials and guarantees

Use testimonials and guarantees anywhere and everywhere in your copy. Provide information to ensure they're credible. For testimonials, use the person's name, their company name if relevant, their city if you operate on a national or international basis, and if you can, a photo. Some of your customers may be uncomfortable with this, so it should be completely optional.

Equally, don't hide your guarantee in the small print. State it proudly as a condition of doing business with you. Show your prospects clearly how they will come out of their dealings with you – advantaged and protected.

Is your website sticky?

Building a successful online business gives you the freedom to focus on more important things while your website earns revenue. To ensure that can happen, there are three key areas to concentrate on – the content of your site, attracting visitors and capturing their details when they get there.

When visitors land on your homepage, is your web copy compelling enough to make them stay and read what you have to say?

Less than 1 per cent of website visitors take any action. Let me say that again. Less than 1 per cent of all the visitors who land on your website will contact you, bookmark your site, subscribe to your newsletter or make a purchase. And once they've gone, they may never come back. So you must provide compelling reasons for them to hand over their contact details.

Customers are just like you

Think how you use the internet yourself. In the last few days you may have made a couple of online purchases, and they were probably purchases of things you've bought before or buy regularly. The majority of your time online is spent finding information – researching potential purchases, reviewing the competition, checking your bank account, etc. So why would your prospective customers behave any differently?

Is your website useful?

Even if your website is 100 per cent commerce, it must also be a source of high-quality information about your area of expertise. This could include downloadable reports, copies of your press releases, product reviews, top tips and even competitions. Customers often don't know what questions to ask (remember the last time you had to make a purchase you knew very little about), and this inevitably makes them nervous and uncomfortable. So help them out by explaining the benefits, the application, the value, the ways to get best results, comparison of brand, etc.

Are you capturing your visitors?

As so few visitors will stay long enough to really read the content of your website, you must attempt to capture email addresses at every opportunity so that you can keep in touch with them and build the relationship directly. Newsletters are very common now and don't often form a strong enough reason in themselves, so in order to get your visitors to hand over their details, make sure you are offering valuable information in the form of reviews and reports. Newsletters shouldn't be disregarded completely, though, as they are an excellent way to keep in touch regularly with visitors.

The opt-in approaches you use on your website are also a great way for visitors to self-qualify their interest. For example, if you are a financial adviser, visitors downloading information on repairing adverse credit will be looking for a different relationship from those who download advice on buying overseas property.

Is it easy to buy from you?

Another point to remember when visitors are navigating your website is your ordering process. Are you making it difficult for people to buy from you? A look at your shopping cart abandonment rate will give you an indication of current statistics, and your hosting company can help with this.

When you've got that elusive customer all the way from information to ordering to checkout, how can you increase their order as much as possible? Point of sale purchases work in the real world and are equally successful in the online world. You can introduce a linked system that shows 'other customers who bought XYZ also bought…', or if your business is less focused on online sales, you can ensure there are constant reminders of your full offering throughout the website.

Do you stay in touch?

And if it wasn't daunting enough to collect all those email addresses from customers, newsletters, subscribers and visitors who want to hear your news, how do you keep in touch afterwards, without employing half a dozen more staff or having a nervous breakdown? Autoresponders are the answer. A quick search on any of the search engines will present dozens of autoresponder providers, and you can learn more about how these automated message systems work.

Autoresponder is a program that automatically answers emails sent to it. It is often used as an email sales tool to provide information immediately to prospective customers and follow up at preset time intervals. It is also used to issue newsletters to subscribers, capture contact details and send delivery confirmations.

Keep an eye on your visitors

Do you have accurate statistics on your current website visitor numbers? Whilst a simple visitor counter is useful, it is much more beneficial to understand the path your visitors follow through your site, the time they spend there and the links they click.

If you don't already track the path that visitors to your website take, you could try a package like **www.statisfy.com**, which is completely free and easy to understand. Simply add the code provided to the code of your website and watch the journey that your site surfers take.

Among the elements you may want to test is banner advertising – the adverts that run across the top of a web page. These often are considered appropriate only to big companies, but they could really work for your business. By testing headlines and offers in pay per click, you'll know what generates the best response and you can trial banner advertising. Always ensure your advertising is 'direct response' – that is, asking visitors to click for a specific purpose, instead of just in the hope that they'll like your site.

The biggest error (revisited)

I must warn you once more about the one big mistake that the majority of businesses continue to make – making your core message about you rather than about your customers.

Step into your audience's shoes and think about the information from their perspective, and you will have the key to successful business copywriting. It has the added advantage of feeding into your face-to-face communications, as your employees start to become more confident and successful in their customer-facing roles when they use this type of language.

Two examples

To illustrate my point about strong copy, here are two examples of what you might find on a website's homepage. See if you can tell which one makes the big mistake.

Company 1: ABC Design provides effective, stylish and affordable website design and development. As a well established small business web design company, we can offer a range of affordable web design services to any small business or UK company. We have built a strong reputation as a UK website design company by consistently building web pages and producing sites that are good looking, technically excellent and affordable for small businesses and individuals.

Compare this to:

Company 2: XYZ Design specialises in creating unique, exciting and accessible web pages that really allow your business to succeed on the web. Whether you want your website to showcase your business, to sell your products online, or to be database-driven, our web designers can provide carefully tailored solutions for each of these. We aim to provide you with the best service at the highest quality and lowest price. Our website designers will liaise with you at every stage of the web design process. By carefully balancing web page design with structure, we create visually appealing, robust and usable websites that quickly become a tangible asset for your business.

Not difficult, is it? Company 2 matches their technical skills and capabilities with the needs of their audience. They focus on benefits like tangible assets and allowing your business to succeed on the web.

Company 1, on the other hand, briefly mentions affordability, though as we all know, that is a very subjective concept. But mainly, they talk about themselves. And I can hazard a confident guess that that approach will continue through all their marketing materials.

With the greatest respect to all the entrepreneurs reading this book and our excellent, noble companies, our customers just don't care about us. Let's now take a look at how we can make sure our ads and sales messages reflect what they *do* care about.

Guidelines for getting your message across

When committing your business vision to print, here are some guidelines to help you on your way:

→ *Your main message must be the most prominent.* Don't be tempted to devote half the space to a striking picture. The biggest part of the advert must be your main benefit statement. This is the part that entices the audience to keep reading.

→ *Offer a single impressive benefit, quickly and simply.* Research proves that the best adverts are those which offer an impressive, relevant benefit to the reader. This 'promise' should ideally contain the business brand name, take no longer than about 4–8 seconds to read, be about 11 to 15 words, and be clearly the most striking part of the advert. You must keep it quick, simple and to the point. Think about the vocabulary and language you use – know your target audience.

→ *Your message must be quick and easy to absorb.* Use a clear layout, clear fonts and clear language. Don't distract the reader from the text with images or fancy fonts. Use simple language, avoid complicated words and keep enough space around the text to attract attention to it. Use simple traditional serif fonts in 10, 11 or 12 point size for the main text in magazines and newspapers; smaller or larger are actually more difficult to read and therefore less likely to be read.

→ *Involve the reader in your writing style.* Refer to the audience as 'you' and use the second person ('you', 'your' and 'yours', etc.) in the description of what your business does for the customer to get them visualising their own personal involvement. Describe the service as it affects them, in a way that they will easily relate to it.

→ *Develop an offering that is special or unique*. Why should people be interested if your proposition is no different from your competition? Emphasise what makes your service special and new. Unless your code of practice prevents you from claiming superiority over your competitors, you should put as much emphasis as you can behind your USP (unique selling point), and either imply or state directly that you are the only company to offer these things.

→ *Your offer must be credible and believable*. The Advertising Standards Authority would prevent you from making overly extravagant claims anyway, but you should make your offer seem perfectly credible. Explaining 'why' and 'how' you are able to do the things you are offering overcomes huge psychological barriers in the prospective buyer's mind.

→ *Use lower case type*. Word-shapes are lost when capitals are used. People read by recognising word-shapes not individual letters, so don't use capital letters for text, and ideally not for headlines either, as it takes longer to read and reduces impact.

→ *Headlines should be three-quarters up the page or advert space*. Position your headline statement where it can be seen quickly. Do not put headlines at the very top of the space. The eye is naturally drawn to between two-thirds and three-quarters up the page or space, which is where the main benefit statement needs to be.

What not to do

It's just as easy to succeed as to fail in indirect selling, so here are a few simple guidelines of what not to do. You'll probably still find lots of other mistakes to make on your own – but at least you won't have to make these.

Not knowing your audience

Every ad should be to a specific targeted group that you research until you know it intimately. Aim for your readers' personal hot spots, in a writing style and level they're comfortable with. Learn how they feel and act and what they like and dislike. Then craft your style and content specifically to your readership.

Mailing to the wrong list

This is probably the most common, and most fatal, error made in mailings. Spend as much time on researching your list as you do on the creative aspects of writing and layout and on the research about your products, pricing and offer. Unless the people on your mailing list want or need your product or service, they'll be tough to convince and probably impossible to sell to. If you can't afford to lose the money, make sure you find the time for this.

Lack of clear objectives

Nothing blurs good writing like not having a specific goal. Make sure you know where you're going with each piece you write, and stay focused. Write your objective first, in the upper right-hand corner of your page, and refer to it often. Stay on target.

Price before offer

'Only £49.95!' No matter what you're selling, a price has no meaning until readers know what they're getting. Make sure you tell them about your product first. If your number one sales point is your product's low price, you may introduce the price early on in the same sentence. Bear in mind, though, that the price is almost never the exclusive selling point.

Price before benefits

'Just £89.95!' may sound like a great price to you for a stereo, but if you present it first – before showing exactly how great the product is – most of your readers will bin your brochure before they even see your offer. You need to tell them what makes your price so great in terms of benefits (i.e. what's in it for them).

Wrong price point

There are thousands of theories on how to price your product correctly. However, each formula gives you a different answer. There's only one absolutely certain way to set your price – let the market decide. You do this by testing each price point you think will work, and then seeing which one brings in not only the most orders, but also the most overall profit. That's your price. Simple, isn't it?

Inadequate testing

There's no reason to lose big money in direct mail. Everything is testable, and you should test small mailings until one is clearly a winner. Then ramp up slowly. Next time, mail to a slightly larger test group. If that works, test still larger mailings. Until you know you're absolutely going to be profitable, just stick with smaller test mailings so you'll never lose big money. How will you know you'll be successful? As long as you mail the same package to the same list, your results should be the same. Your advertising has a fixed cost whether it brings you three leads or 300, so you owe it to yourself to get the best possible return for your investment.

Wrong objective

Asking for the sale instead of starting the relationship can be a fatal mistake. The objective of a small ad or direct mail piece is to get the prospect to call, write in, email, visit your website or whatever you want them to do. Your objective should be to get the reader to call for additional information (or for your free informational booklet, free report, free sample, etc.). Generally, you do not ask for the sale in an ad or a short letter; you ask for an action. Then, offer the product, show the benefits, educate, inform and create the desire.

Wrong headline

The headline is the single most important element of your ad. Solely on the basis of this one line, your reader makes the decision to continue reading – or not to. Write 100 headlines, then pick the best one. (Sounds excessive, but it really works, I promise.) Spend several days on this task.

Not telling your readers exactly what you want them to do

You should tell your readers several times exactly what you want them to do. Be specific. Let readers know exactly what action you want them to take; tell them, and tell them again. Aim for four times, but a really well-written piece could state the action ten times.

Forgetting the PS

A PS at the foot of the page is the second most read part of a direct mail letter after the headline. Use it to reiterate your sales message – it will get read.

Unethical behaviour

Always be very clear about the opt-out procedures for recipients and stick to them.

The six golden rules

Here are the six golden rules of great business copywriting. These are the big concepts to keep in mind every time you write any kind of sales copy.

Rule 1: Benefits

The start, the middle and the end of great copy that gets your reader itching to buy from you has to focus on the benefits that they will experience. By stating the benefits, you force yourself to write from your customers' perspective. Whatever it is they buy from you – be it safety, speed, comfort, luxury, relaxation, professionalism, security, skills, profitability, wealth – make sure you state it in everything you write.

Rule 2: 'You' and 'your'

All your communications should be a dialogue, not a monologue. As if to prove my point, you are probably reading those words and thinking 'How can it be a dialogue? My words are in print.' But I am asking you questions and talking to you as if you were sitting across the room from me. And hopefully my questions (that your subconscious mind has to answer – remember?) will cause you to answer aloud occasionally, as if I were in the room with you.

Sometimes it is very easy to get caught up in the fabulous detail of the business we run, the products we offer, the machinery and equipment we have invested in or the number of happy, loyal staff who are working alongside us. But you must force yourself to write for your customers.

Rule 3: Positioning

Al Ries and Jack Trout, the American sales and marketing gurus, created 22 immutable laws of marketing. In them they stated that you must own a category in people's heads. For example, if I said 'cola drinks' to you, who springs to mind as 'owning' that category? Probably only a couple to choose from, I would guess. What about fast-food burgers? Or filterless vacuums? Or non-stick pans? Or safe cars? Or personal MP3 players?

These are all mass-market consumer products, and I appreciate that your business might not be in that field. But in the world that your company exists in, do you own a category?

If the main category, or the one you'd like to own, is already taken, what do you do? Create your own! Find a category that you can be number one in. And then state it clearly in everything you say.

Rule 4: Leadership

This is often an area that causes untold discomfort amongst business entrepreneurs in the UK – the idea of being a leader or an expert. What if no one has told you that you're the expert yet? Well, you'll be waiting a little while if you won't claim leadership until someone else says so. So make it true. Lead with your opinions, your advice, your style, your marketing. Be bold. Unless your company is in one of the few remaining categories where competition rules forbid you from stating expertise or leadership, you should commit to it 100 per cent.

If you can back up your leadership with statistics and figures, that's even better. But if your starting point is simply to say 'We are the leading experts in…', start there and make it true.

Customers want to trust their supplier, and creating that rapport is much easier when you feel you're buying from someone who really knows their stuff.

Rule 5: Take care with pricing

I touched on pricing in Chapter Two. And now I'm going to say it again, clearly, so you never forget. Your pricing has a very significant psychological impact on the way your customers perceive you. There are implicit messages in price reductions and low prices. Those messages are the absolute, diametric opposite to leadership.

Pricing is a huge factor in your unintended communications, because it says, 'We don't believe in ourselves or our products enough to charge what they're worth.'

It's very likely that your customers are not buying solely on price. Do you? Really? So you only ever buy the cheapest brands, grow your food in the garden, walk to work and wear handmade clothes? No, I didn't think so.

Not having enough money very rarely stops us from buying something we want. If we want or need it enough, we find the money. What stops us is not seeing the value in it. If you are worried that your prices won't match your competitors, increase your prices and try adding bonuses to the value of the original discount instead.

Rule 6: Call to action

People like to be led. Not against their will, and not to anything harmful or illegal. But think how comforting it is when someone with authority, an expert in their field perhaps, advises you, supports you, points out the things you might have missed.

Our customers are asking us to take them by the hand so that they're not confused and they don't end up wasting time or money. Make it easy for them. Be specific and clear about the action you want them to take. Really spell it out for them. And say it more than once.

The basic process for your copywriting could take this outline:

→ Define the action you want your readers to take.

→ List the benefits that whatever you are offering will give to them.

→ Determine what people who do not have what you are offering may be curious about in regard to it.

→ Create your headline or title from the most compelling benefit or point of curiosity you have listed.

→ Create a desire to know based on the points of curiosity you listed and show the benefits people will receive upon taking the action you defined.

→ Call for them to take that action.

Web bonus

At our website, **www.forentrepreneursbooks.com**, click on the 'Selling for Entrepreneurs' button. On the link for Chapter Nine you can download templates to get you started on some of the most common forms of indirect sales, including advertisements and mailers.

Key points

→ Indirect sales – written or other non-verbal information – continues to sell when you can't physically be there with your prospect.

→ Adverts, mailers, websites and letters all use more sophisticated techniques than ever to support the natural buying process.

→ Writing strong sales copy is a learned skill – the more you do it, the better you'll get.

→ Avoiding the major writing pitfalls that most businesses make will give you a clear head start.

Next steps

What action will you take to apply the information in this chapter? By when will you do it?

_____

_____

_____

_____

The secrets of selling

Part Three

AIDA

Chapter Ten

AIDA describes the basic process by which people become motivated to act on external stimulus, including the way that successful selling happens and sales are made. AIDA stands for:

Attention

Interest

Desire

Action

This is the process that buyers work through and sellers must follow. As your prospect moves through the sales funnel process, the information they need and receive from you will focus on different parts of the AIDA process.

The AIDA process also applies to any advertising or communication that aims to generate a response, and it provides a reliable template for the design of all sorts of business material.

Simply, when we sell something we must sell through the AIDA stages. Something first gets our **attention**. If it's relevant to us we are **interested** to learn or hear more about it. If the product or service then appears to closely match our needs and/or aspirations and resources, particularly if it is special, unique or rare, we begin to **desire** it. If we are prompted or stimulated to overcome our natural caution we may then become motivated or susceptible to taking **action** to buy.

The power of questions

At every point in the AIDA process – giving our attention, becoming interested, desiring the product or service and taking the decision to act on our desire – we need to feel we are learning. We have questions that need answering, and we expect the other person to have questions of us.

Questions are incredibly powerful things. Your subconscious mind has to answer them. Have you ever been asked who played a role in a particular film, or where you last saw the Philips-head screwdriver, and suffered that nagging feeling that you know the answer, but you just can't remember? Your subconscious mind will keep searching until it can present a satisfactory response, however long that takes.

This is one of the reasons I gave in Chapter Two as to why you should never ask yourself poor quality questions like 'Why does this always happen to me?' or 'How come other people are better at selling than I am?' Your subconscious mind will relentlessly seek out the answer to prove that you're right.

The same benefit can address completely different emotional needs in different prospects. A common example of this is in the car showroom. The salesperson could show the same car to two people, but address two completely different emotional needs, for speed, power and exhilaration or for safety, reliability and control. Both needs are met by the same benefit of the car's powerful engine and state-of-the-art brakes.

Effective selling involves very little selling. Music to the ears of those reluctant sellers, I know. But what I mean is that customers buy for their own reasons, not for the reasons you think they should. So the hard sell focused on the wrong need is time wasted for everybody.

Instead of focusing on selling, you need to be asking lots of excellent questions, which in turn will help your prospect to actually make the buying decisions by themselves.

Selling is like dating (in a manner of speaking, you understand). Both parties are keen to know as much as possible about the other, to see whether there is any reason for them to meet again. Unfortunately, many salespeople feel that they are selling when they just respond to their prospect's questions. They mistakenly believe this will demonstrate how smart or knowledgeable they are and will help their prospect make a buying decision. Naturally, the prospect doesn't always know the right questions to ask. They don't know what they don't know. And simply answering their questions can leave them with a false impression, for better or worse.

The right and wrong questions

Many salespeople have learned to ask questions, and all too often they sound like this:

'If I could save you money, would you be interested?'
'Is this the one you want?'
'What will it take to earn your business?'

The problem with questions like these is that they do not help you gain the knowledge you need to effectively present a solution. They only demonstrate a lack of sales ability that will quickly cause the prospect to lose interest in the call or discussion.

Instead, you need to ask good quality questions that will make your prospect think and will demonstrate your company's knowledge and expertise. Learn more about the prospect's goals and challenges and you will gain more insight to your prospect's business. And this means you will be able to present an attractive solution.

Seek first to understand, then to be understood – always aim for the Win-Win. STEPHEN COVEY

AIDA in action

AIDA, in practice within your business, could look like this.

Attention

Getting the other person's attention sets the tone. First impressions count. Getting attention is more difficult than it used to be, because people are less accessible, have less free time and have lots of competing distractions, so think about when it's best to call.

Gimmicks, tricks and crafty techniques don't work, because your prospective customers, just like the rest of us, are irritated by hundreds of them every day.

If you are calling on the phone or meeting face to face you have about five seconds to attract attention, by which time the other person has formed their first impression of you. Despite the time pressure, relax and enjoy it. Smile, people can hear it in your voice. Sit upright, with your chin off your chest, and ensure that somewhere in your eye line is a motivational statement, inspiring image or other positive reinforcement tool.

Interest

You now have maybe 5–15 seconds in which to create some interest. Something begins to look interesting if it is relevant and potentially advantageous.

This implies a lot. The person you are approaching should have a potential need for your product or service or proposition (which implies that you or somebody else has established a target customer profile).

You must approach the other person at a suitable time (i.e. when it's convenient), and that means aspects of seasonality and other factors affecting timing have been taken into account.

You must empathise with and understand the other person's situation and issues, and be able to express yourself in their terms (i.e. talk their language).

Desire

The salesperson needs to be able to identify and acknowledge the prospect's situation, needs, priorities and constraints on personal and organisational levels, through empathic questioning and interpretation.

You must build rapport and trust, and also a preparedness in the prospect's mind to do business with you personally (thus dispelling the prospect's feelings of doubt or risk about your own integrity and ability).

You must understand your competitors' capabilities and your prospect's other options. You must obviously understand your product (specification, options, features and benefits), and particularly all relevance and implications for your prospect. You must be able to present, explain and convey solutions with credibility and enthusiasm.

My golden nugget here is to ask, 'What is most important to you about…?' And then be quiet and let them talk. Let them tell you all the needs they want met, all the problems they have currently and the way they want you to sell to them.

The key is being able to demonstrate how you, your own organisation and your product will suitably, reliably and sustainably 'match' the prospect's needs identified and agreed, within all constraints.

Creating desire is part skill and technique and part behaviour and style. In modern selling and business, trust and relationship (the 'you' factor) are increasingly significant, as natural competitive development inexorably squeezes and reduces the opportunities for clear product advantage and uniqueness.

Action

This is the conversion of potential into actuality, to achieve or move closer to whatever is the aim. Natural inertia and caution often dictate that clear opportunities are not acted upon, particularly by purchasers of all sorts, so the salesperson must suggest, or encourage agreement, that they move to complete the sale or move to the next stage.

The better the preceding three stages have been conducted, the less emphasis is required for the action stage; in fact, on a few rare occasions a sale is so well conducted that the prospect decides to take action without any encouragement at all.

Every question you ask should potentially move the prospect on to the next stage of the sales funnel. Remember, you're not trying to get the sale, you're just trying to determine whether you should make plans for a second date.

Combining AIDA and powerful questions

Here are three tips to help develop good quality sales questions to use at every stage of the AIDA process.

1 Determine your key objective

What information do you require in order to move the sales process forward or determine the best solution for your customer? Your questions will vary depending on the customer.

2 Consider the person you will be speaking with

The higher up you go in an organisation, the more strategic your questions need to be. Questions about the company's goals and objectives and the challenges and barriers that are preventing them from reaching those targets will give you valuable insight.

3 Use 'what' questions

What caused that problem? What action are you taking to achieve your goals? What specific challenges are preventing you from reaching your targets? What results are you expecting? By determining the cause of their problems, you will be able to better tailor your presentation and show your prospect how your product or service is a solution.

With those in mind, now let's see how such questions fit into each stage of the AIDA process.

The Attention stage

First you must strive to get your prospect's attention. Without attention, you can hardly persuade them of anything. You can get attention in many ways, and a good way is to surprise them.

When you are talking to them, the first few seconds are essential as they will listen most then and rapidly decide whether you are worth giving further attention. Don't waste these precious moments. Grab the other person's attention immediately. Keep in your mind that they will mentally be asking, 'Why should I listen to you?'

It is better to open with something that pulls them towards you rather than something that scares them (as this may push them away).

Good quality questions in the Attention stage address the prospect's problems and are almost always open ended, such as:

'Have you ever...?'
'Are you noticing...?'
'Can you see...?'

Poor quality questions give them something to object to, demonstrate your disrespect or just bore them to tears. They may sound like this:

'Do you know the features of our new...?'
'I was only wondering whether you could give me...?'
'Do you know what I was saying to X about…?'

The Interest stage

Once you have their attention, sustain it by getting the other person interested. Watch out for the boredom factor. You may be able to get someone interested, but you cannot expect to keep their attention for ever. Try questions that help them visualise a potential new world for themselves or their business:

'Could you get excited about...?'
'Do you see the benefit in...?'
'Are you looking forward to...?'
'Doesn't it make sense to...?'
'Do you know how many people...?'
'Isn't it about time...?'
'What do you imagine...?'
'How often have you been...?'

The Desire stage

Once they are interested in you and what you have to say, the next step is to create a desire in them for what you want them to do. They can recognise that they have a need, but this is not desire. Desire is a motivation to act and leads towards the next stage.

At this point, your questions need to become more specific, helping the prospect to crystallise any issues they are facing:

'I notice you currently use XYZ Company. How long have they been your supplier?'
'What do you like most about them?'
'If you could change one aspect about your current arrangement, what would it be?'
'What are the most important issues for you?'
'What have your experiences been with ABC?'
'Where do you see your greatest challenge?'

The Action stage

This is the magic stage, when they take action on their desires and actually buy the product or agree to your proposals. Listen to the signals they are sending. Are they asking you about when you can deliver or what after-sales support you give?

The questions you use at this stage can be quite specific to the particular buying environment of your product, and this is traditionally the stage that 'closing' questions come into their own. For example:

'Would you like me to arrange delivery to this office or directly to the branch?'

'Would you prefer the pay-as-you-go option or the unlimited monthly usage?'

When you combine such questions with the cutting-edge methods outlined in the next chapter, your sales power will be even greater.

Key points

→ Knowing everything about your product won't get you the sale. Neither will knowing every detail of your company's history.

→ Prospects work through Attention–Interest–Desire–Action, and your questions will help them move through these stages.

→ Our subconscious mind has to answer a question, and better quality questions get better quality answers.

→ Effective selling involves very little of what is traditionally regarded as sales.

→ Creating great questions will ensure you move the prospects that need moving and discount the ones that need discounting.

Next steps

What action will you take to apply the information in this chapter? By when will you do it?

_____

_____

_____

_____

Influencing people and hypnotic sales

Chapter Eleven

You owe it to yourself and your business to be an excellent communicator, influencer and sales professional. One of the most immediate changes you can make to a business is to improve the communication and influencing skills of the key players. Building rapport and influencing behaviour are often seen as 'gifts', but this chapter sets out clearly how everyone can develop the skills and put them into action.

There is no right way, nor is there only one way to influence others. Everything, but everything, is a factor when influencing people. And we are, all of us, influenced by people, places, events and situations at all times. Sometimes we are affected more or less by these things, but we are continually being influenced by what happens around us.

All human influence is powerful, and the skills that you'll hone will be just as applicable to your personal life as to your business. Consider it an extra bonus from me that you'll develop the ability to influence the behaviour and decisions of your children or your partner!

In other words

Neuro Linguistic Programming (NLP) is a theory of language, communication and thought, which holds that people can improve the way they interact with the world by means of certain principles and techniques concerned with their use of language.

The role of influence

Your job requires you to influence people just about all of the time. It may take the form of gaining support, inspiring others, persuading other people to become your champions, engaging someone's imagination or creating relationships. Whatever form it takes, being an excellent influencer makes your job easier.

An interesting point about people who use their influencing skills well is that other people like being around them. There's a kind of exciting buzz, or a sense that things happen when they're about. It's because they don't sit around wishing things were different while moaning there's nothing they can do about it. It's also because we all like to feel part of something, and we love to feel involved. Great influencers help everyone around them to take action and achieve results.

Truly excellent influencing skills require a healthy combination of interpersonal communication, presentation and assertiveness techniques. It is about adapting and modifying your personal style when you become aware of the effect you are having on other people, while still being true to yourself. Behaviour and attitude change are what's important, not changing who you are or how you feel and think. As some of the great American influencers and motivators of the last century say, how you feel doesn't change what you do, it's what you do that affects how you feel.

What it isn't

You may try to exert your influence through coercion and manipulation. You might even succeed in getting things done, but that isn't really influencing. That's forcing people to do what you want, often against their will. You won't have succeeded in winning support.

Pushing, bullying, bludgeoning or haranguing don't work. And neither does manipulation. Like elephants, people will remember the experience.

Indeed, if you force someone to do something you want, without taking their point of view into consideration, the impression that person is left with is how they will see you for ever. You're stuck with it, unless you deliberately change what you do in order to be seen differently.

And this is the traditional image of sales – an adversarial stand-off where there was a winner and a loser, and the salesman lost his commission if he was the loser.

Being entirely honest with oneself is a good exercise.

SIGMUND FREUD

What it is

People are far more willing to come halfway (or more) if they feel acknowledged, understood and appreciated. They may even end up doing or agreeing to something they wouldn't previously have done because they feel good about making the choice.

Have you ever bought something you hadn't intended to, not because the sales assistant forced you into it, but rather because they persuaded you that your choice would be a good one?

Influencing is about understanding yourself and the effect or impact you have on others. Though it can, on occasion, be one-way, the primary relationship is two-way, and it is about changing how others perceive you. In other words, the cliché, perception is reality, makes perfect sense in the context of influencing.

It doesn't matter what's going on internally for you. If it isn't perceived by the other person, then it doesn't exist, other than in your mind. You could be doing the most brilliant presentation you've ever done, but if you haven't brought your 'audience' with you, the brilliance is wasted. And that's about being able to see what's going on for them, which will be different, however much you may have in common. Sometimes you can get so used to your own personal style or way of being or pattern of communicating that you don't think of how it is being received, and you don't think of behaving in any other way.

Influencing can sometimes be looked at as the ability to 'finesse', almost sleight of hand. The other person isn't prodded into seeing your view of the world, but is persuaded, often unconsciously, into understanding it.

Influencing is about being able to move things forward, without pushing, forcing or telling others what to do.

When you attempt to influence others, especially in a selling environment, there is a pathway you must follow that replicates the human emotional process.

You and your role in influencing

This path starts with your own beliefs about the situation, the prospect, your products and services, and yourself. If your basic mindset is in the wrong place, you won't take the required action to ensure that your customers benefit from your products and services. The beliefs you hold about yourself, your business, your offering and your customers will impact on your words and actions. This includes your beliefs about selling itself and the selling process.

In the UK, there are clear accepted beliefs about the culture of selling. These beliefs often centre on the thought that anyone who sells is dodgy and underhanded, untrustworthy and generally to be watched at all times. That perception probably makes you nervous and uncomfortable about having to sell.

Your willingness to take action on everything within this book relates to your passionate belief that it is a good thing to sell to your customers. If the driving force of your business is the desire to add value to the lives of your customers, and it should be, then the selling process is simply the relationship you develop with customers and prospects that allows them to experience that value.

This is particularly relevant for the sale of intangibles and the service associated with the sale of products. You owe it to your customers and prospects to inform them about the opportunities you offer and the needs you meet, and let them decide if this is something they want.

The relationship

People buy things based on emotion and rationalise their decision later. When you create rapport with your customers and prospects, you start to build trust and comfort, which breaks down the barriers to sale. But creating rapport sounds like an ideal. How do you achieve it?

You can actually create rapport with someone within a few seconds of meeting them the first time, using a clever technique that was uncovered during a study of successful therapists and how they created such a bond with their patients. The technique is called mirroring, and it involves you physically replicating someone else's gestures, posture, speech patterns and volume, body language and movements.

If you're anything like me, you probably read that last paragraph with something approaching doubt or dismissal. But think back to a conversation you've had with someone you did not know well, but where you felt at ease and comfortable without being certain why. Chances are the other person was consciously or unconsciously mirroring you. Our brains look for things that resonate with us – that are similar, reassuring and attractive. By adopting someone else's posture, movements and vocal speed, you demonstrate that you have empathy with them, and that you are adopting their mindset and perspective. This is particularly important in a sales situation, where you want to show quickly that you have respect for your prospect.

You certainly shouldn't attempt to copy the other person identically or in any way that makes either of you uncomfortable, but this simple technique will help the conversation to go more smoothly for you both.

Mirroring is even more important on the phone, when someone cannot see your body language or mannerisms. By adopting the other person's voice speed, volume and words or phrases, you will put them at ease.

Roger realised he'd gone one step too far in mirroring the customer.

Questions again

Although you have demonstrated to your prospect that you respect them and see their point of view by mirroring them, you aren't a mind-reader and you should never guess or assume how your offering matches their needs.

People want to buy from you. But to do that, they want you to present your offering in a way they can feel emotionally. If your business is more than just you, I urge you to be absolutely certain (by asking smart questions) that everyone who has any interaction whatsoever with your customers is aware of the role they play within the influencing process.

Body language

In studies, it has repeatedly been shown that the words you use are only a part of your overall impact and influencing potential. The tone, volume and speed of your voice are also important, as are your physiology, your body language and your gestures. And that is not completely undone when you're on the phone – the other person can still 'hear' your body language and gestures. If you are slumped in your chair, looking down, with the phone jammed between your ear and your shoulder, the words you use will always be less powerful.

These 'unintended' communications can make or break a sale or a customer relationship.

Always be sincere, even if you don't mean it.

HARRY TRUMAN

One of the areas where my studies have focused over the years is the distinctions and differences between businesspeople in different countries and cultures. My experience has found that, as a sweeping generalisation, American businesspeople have stronger influencing skills because they have more powerful and dynamic body language. Where it is common for us Brits to express our discomfort or unease in a sales situation by standing very rigidly, American businesspeople give the impression of being much more relaxed. And this means better sales volume.

Cause and effect

This is an established theory that has been tried and tested in various situations over the centuries (see page 106). But there is a key element that is often overlooked. To achieve the same ultimate effect, you must replicate the causes. In other words, if you want to be successful, you can model what someone else who already is successful is doing, but this often requires more than running a similar advert, adapting someone's script or modifying an existing brochure. It involves adopting the same mindset, the same view of our customers and the same beliefs about ourselves and our businesses.

Selling and sales training ideas, courses, programmes and products are just part of the picture. Modern selling requires understanding and capabilities that extend way beyond traditional 'sales training' skills.

Modern selling is about life, people, business (and increasingly ethical business and corporate responsibility), communications, behaviour, personality and psychology, self-awareness, attitude and belief. Selling is about understanding how people and systems work and enabling good outcomes. And by 'systems' I mean organisations and processes and relationships, not just systems in the sense of tools and IT. Sales training, of course, addresses some of these issues, but not all of them.

The more you understand about how people think, how organisations work and how they are managed, the more effective you will be.

The laws of persuasion

Robert Cialdini, the world-renowned social psychologist, wrote a book called *Influence: Science and Practice*. In it, he highlights the 'laws' of influence and persuasion.

Three of those laws that are particularly relevant to sales are reciprocity, scarcity and social proof. Each of these laws details how people collectively can be influenced into decisions and opinions.

The law of reciprocity

The law of reciprocity says that we all have an inbuilt desire to repay what other people do for us. This is a very important concept for permission marketing (that is, getting people to agree to be marketed to) and the idea of giving away free samples, trial periods, information or reports.

The law of scarcity

The law of scarcity says that things instantly become more appealing when they are less available. This is as true of objects and information as it is of people. When things are perceived as less available, they become more valuable. People are more motivated by the prospect of losing something valuable than by gaining something valuable. Imagine someone told you that you could win £10,000 by entering a competition – you might enter, but you might not. But if they said that you might lose £10,000 by not entering, you would probably feel much more inclined to fill in the entry form.

The law of social proof

The law of social proof says that we decide what is good for us (in the sense of healthy, valuable, useful, interesting, etc.) based on other people's decisions. Think about the 'social proof' that accompanies the latest blockbuster movie. Or those expensive trainers that your child really wants, and everybody else has got (apparently!). Or some new piece of technology that is revolutionising the lives of everyone who has it – for example, iPods, broadband, plasma screen televisions and so on. If you can create the same kind of social proof for your products and services, exploiting the full potential in your testimonials and referrals, you will experience the incredible 'snowball' effect that practically does all your selling for you.

This is where the true entrepreneur stands apart from the masses. Entrepreneurial sellers recognise that spotting the trends and striving to be at the front of customers' minds is more valuable than other businesses ever understand. What are the trends in your industry? How can you create scarcity and social proof in some or all of what you sell?

Know and use your prospects' filters

Today's seller also acknowledges and embraces everybody's differences. Just as our American cousins might seem to adopt the selling role more naturally than us Brits, our customers see the world from their own point of view, with their own filters and preconceptions. We all have our own beliefs and experiences that influence our decisions every day. These filters in themselves might mean that we find an American sales style uncomfortable or fake, in comparison to a 'softer' British approach.

We all have a language base – a way of expressing ourselves and our world in a way that makes sense to us. When others use the same language as we do, we find we 'click' with them much more easily.

Three customers might show that they understand the benefits of your offering in completely different ways – one might say 'I see what you mean', whilst another could say 'that sounds about right' and a third might say 'that feels good'.

The first would be a visual person, who 'sees' what you are saying. Using picture words will help this customer to see your point of view and visualise the outcome.

The second person is likely to be auditory. They can 'hear' ideas and can tell if a proposition is sound. Using sound-based words and phrases will make this person happy.

And the third person is probably described as kinaesthetic, and they are most likely to be in touch with their feelings. They are more comfortable when they can relate to the idea being floated. They appreciate words that create the feelings they want to enjoy, be it comfort, security or relaxation.

How can you know when a customer first approaches your counter or calls your office that they prefer one type of language structure to another? Well, you can't! But what you can do is structure your sales scripts and language to include elements of visual, auditory and kinaesthetic language, and appeal to all your audiences.

By 'painting a picture' of the prospect using your product or service, you can describe what they would see or hear and how they would feel. Let me give you an example. Sit back and read this piece as though you were reading it in a glossy magazine:

Imagine. You look out of your office window on a cold, wintry day. Snow is falling and settling in a crisp, white blanket on the ground. The temperature is still dropping. You have to drive over to see a prospective client.

A big contract depends on you getting there on time.

You smile as you say to yourself, 'I'm glad I bought that XYZ four-wheel drive last week.'

You walk out to the car park; all the sound is muffled by the snow lying on the roads, trees and bushes surrounding your office. You open the car door and slide into the luxurious, soft cream leather seat. The door closes, whisper quiet, matching the peaceful ambience created by the snow.

You switch on the ignition. The engine gives a quick roar as you touch the accelerator. A touch of the button and you feel the car starting to warm. The powerful, smooth wipers glide across and quickly clear the front and rear screens...

Do you suddenly want a new car? And snow? It's powerful, isn't it?

Be careful how you employ these techniques. The language must still flow and make sense to your prospect. And although we have our preferred language style, we use words and phrases from the other categories, too.

Words you can use

Below are dozens of examples of phrases that you can start to include in your sales language, either verbally or in writing. These hypnotic sentence starters will guide and trigger your prospect's emotions, feelings, memories and imagination in order to persuade them to buy your product:

After a moment or two has elapsed...

After you read this next statement you may vividly remember...

And as you are continuing to read this...

And as you are dreaming about...

And as you dream in this information you'll...

And as you do, just notice how...

Keep all that you have read locked in your mind, the letters, words, meanings, and think about them (often, every day, etc.)...

Keep your mind fixed on...

Know in your mind now that you will be able to...

Learn to trust your subconscious mind because...

Less and less you realise...

Let me ask this, if you...?

Let me remind you...

Let the (fears, worries, pain, etc.) drop out of your life...

Let these thoughts go to the back of your mind...

Let those thoughts go deep into the back of your mind...

Nothing is beyond the power of your subconscious mind. Your problems will...

Notice any difference?

Notice as you concentrate...

Visualise your problem as being a...

Visualise yourself being...

You can really let go of what you don't need in your...

You can see more clearly what...

Your conscious mind may doubt or question your subconscious mind, but you will...

Your mind has thought about it for (time period)…

You notice how every word persuades you more and more...

You now become aware of...

You probably didn't read everything, but you paid attention to...

You, through your own conscious and actions, can...

You will allow yourself to accept these suggestions because...

You will be able to go through the day more...

You will be able to recall a great deal of information about...

You will be able to release yourself from...

Those are all very well as sentence starters, I hear you say, but how do I make the rest of the conversation flow? Regular transitions or copy connectors keep your words flowing together. Hypnotic transitions do the same thing but trigger your prospect's imagination and appeal to their subconscious mind. Here are a few examples:

As you imagine...

As well as you recall...

Likewise remember...

Likewise think...

Finally experience...

To finalise, you observe...

First you experience...

Second you visualise...

Third, fantasise...

Last of all you picture...

Suppose that you remember...

Last of all you imagine...

And you recall...

And then you remember...

Or you think...

Either you drift back...

Overwhelmingly you imagine...

Repeatedly you recall...

Of great consequence you think...

To underscore, you envision...

You simply combine a transition with some mind words like imagine, recall, remember, visualise and so on. They can put your prospect into a suggestible state while they're reading or listening.

The relaxation response

One of the most effective ways to open up and persuade your prospect's subconscious mind is to get them to relax first. They will also absorb, store and remember the information easier, which can be good for branding, viral marketing and word-of-mouth marketing.

Another tip for getting your prospects into a flow state is to use a lot of words, phrases and sentences that rhyme. This inevitably feels more comfortable in writing as opposed to spoken words. Haven't you ever read a poem that just flows together and brings your mind along with it?

You can just suggest that your prospect do one or more of the activities below for a few minutes before they read your copy or before they get to an important section of it. It's more effective to suggest a couple of different ways they can relax. They will usually pick the one that works the best. If you only suggest one it might not be the way they like to relax. Even if they only relax a little, it will help open up their subconscious mind. Here are some helpful phrases and activities you could suggest and use:

Remove any distractions before you read this...

Close your eyes and relax for a few minutes...

Focus on a relaxing object for a few minutes...

Remember a relaxing dream you've had...

Allow all your worries to shrink away...

Forget about all your worries and concerns...

Play some soothing music before you read this...

Start to get comfortable...

Take a few minutes to relax and focus on your breathing before you...

Just relax and take a few minutes to unwind...

Imagine hearing one of your favourite relaxing songs...

Settle back in your chair...

Make yourself relaxed and comfortable...

Straighten out a bit and get comfortable...

Take a few minutes to listen to the silence...

Imagine hearing a relaxing sound from Mother Nature...

Visualise a relaxing nature scene...

Empty your mind and re-experience a relaxing time...

Take a few moments to listen to your breathing...

The power of stories

Stories are very hypnotic. When we watch or hear a good story that has a character we would like to be or one that has some similarities to us, we subconsciously place ourselves right into the action of the story.

Your prospects may subconsciously place themselves in your stories, too. Your real, made-up or even non-human characters could be buying your product, enjoying the benefits or being punished for not buying. Anything goes! These words and phrases work well in stories:

Once upon a time...	Last month...
Just the other day...	Last year...
One day...	I was...
Way back in (year)...	My friend was...
Yesterday...	(Character's name) was...
Last week...	It was a...

Commanding prose

You can insert unmarked, embedded commands and benefits within the context of your ad copy. They will go almost unnoticed by your prospect's conscious mind and go straight to their subconscious mind. Here are some examples:

Order now	Handmade
Buy now	Don't miss out
Invest now	Huge selection
Purchase now	Highly regarded
Ask yourself	Fast delivery
Read this	Easy to assemble
Be attractive	Custom-made
A must	Fully automatic

Show you understand

You can tell your readers vague and general things about themselves. The statements should be information that could apply to anyone or just your target audience. This will make your readers feel like you really know and understand them, which will create trust, rapport and credibility. It makes you look almost psychic! Here are some words to use:

I sense you...	You probably feel...
I know you...	You likely see...
I feel you...	I'm sensing that you...
I see you...	I'm seeing that you...
I picture you...	In the present...
I know you...	At times you feel...

Credibility

Sensory persuasion is what you or someone else saw, have seen, heard, felt, tasted, smelled or even sensed. You can use the exact source if you have their permission or, if you don't, you can use a general name, such as book, TV, he, she, experts and so on. They bring credibility to your words because you're not the only one making those statements. Your prospects will trust what you're saying even more. Here's how to phrase it:

I read in (source) that...

I saw on (source) that...

I heard on (source) that...

I heard from (source) that...

(Source) heard...

PS: don't forget the PS

A PS is usually the second thing people read, after the main headline. You must be able to influence your prospects to order before they leave your copy. One way is by complimenting, praising or thanking them for attempting to improve their life or solve their problems, and this is easy and natural to do in a PS, like these:

Selling for Entrepreneurs

I appreciate the time you took to read this ad.

You made a real accomplishment by considering solving your problem today.

I'm impressed with the time you took to read this ad.

You've come a long way at least considering making your life better.

You've got what it takes to improve your life. You just need a little help from us.

I admire you for not being scared to take a risk.

You deserve a lot of credit for changing and taking charge of your life.

You'll really make a difference in your life by ordering.

You really proved you want to better your situation.

You're really intelligent for taking time to read this ad copy.

You're certainly determined to reach your goals.

You won my respect by just reading this ad copy.

You're a winner because you're trying to get over your obstacles.

You've got determination because of your risk-taking attitude.

You've shown me a lot of confidence by just reading this sales letter.

I salute you for taking time out of your busy day to improve your family's life.

Some other complimenting and praising words you can use, in a PS or elsewhere include:

Talented	Educated
Well-educated	Dedicated
Witty	Confident
Seasoned	Ambitious
Resourceful	Risk-taker

Guide their reading

Ask your prospects to read persuasive parts of your ad copy in different ways. When they do this they are using more of their senses to absorb your message. It can then influence their conscious and subconscious mind at the same time. This can quickly help to brand your product and persuade them to buy with their other senses. Some phrases that work this way are:

Mentally ask yourself...

Silently and slowly read...

Visualise each word you mentally read...

Mentally tell yourself...

Tell yourself out loud...

Think about the meaning of each word you read...

Talk to yourself about what you have just read...

Imagine listening to your favourite song as you read...

Sing the following sentence...

Mentally imagine listening to my voice as you read out loud...

From benefit to affirmation

Convert your benefits into subconscious affirmations. As your prospects read them they end up talking to themselves in a positive, present tense. It's like they are persuading themselves to buy your product! Here's how:

I know how to...

I am learning ways to...

I am discovering...

I will uncover...

I am learning strategies...

I'm definitely unlocking...

I know why...

I am finding out tactics...

I am learning benefits...

The ESP strategy

Psychics are thought to have ESP (extrasensory perception). They gather information without using the known five senses (sight, hearing, smell, taste or touch). But they do use information from the regular five senses as evidence to make their final conclusion. The information they acquire can be about a person, a future event, the past and so on.

Many commentators think we all have ESP. They think some people just have a stronger sense than others. They also think you can strengthen the psychic ability you already possess, be it weak or strong.

Have you ever been in a business meeting and finished someone else's words before they did? Have you ever had a positive feeling about a new product and been right? Have you ever known that a colleague was lying to you without having any evidence and then found out you were right?

Or maybe you've had:

→ a 'mental sign', like a light or spark going off in your head, similar to when you suddenly have a good idea;

→ a 'physical sign', like butterflies in your stomach, similar to driving quickly over a hill;

→ an 'emotional sign', like the feeling of excitement, similar to getting a huge tax refund when you weren't expecting it;

→ a 'thought sign', something you can't stop thinking about, similar to getting ready to meet a blind date;

→ a 'visual sign', like mentally seeing an image to write about, similar to seeing an event before it happens.

You don't need to be psychic in order to use psychic phrases in your sales language. You can call your best customers and ask them questions such as 'What other kind of products are you interested in?' or 'What did you like best or least about our product?'

These questions can give you an idea of what kind of products to develop or offer in the future.

Be colourful

As well as powerful words and phrases, you can increase the success of your written, printed or online information by incorporating powerful colours and imagery.

Red

Use red to get people a little extra-excited about your product or service. Use red in headlines and subheadlines because it grabs people's attention. Red stop signs do the same thing. Use red in your closing and when you ask prospects to order. Red can persuade people to take action.

Things people might feel and associate with the colour red are: love, romance, fire, war, blood, roses, danger, fire engines, sex, stop signs, etc.

Yellow

People usually buy more quickly if they're in a good mood. Yellow can create a happy mood. For example, on a sunny day people are usually in a better mood than on a cloudy day.

Things people might feel and associate with the colour yellow are: corn, brightness, cheerfulness, light, idea, lightning, sun, gold, daisies, etc.

Pink

Pink is regarded as a friendly colour. When people are friendly with us, our nature is to be friendly right back (maybe like purchasing a product). Pink makes a good background colour.

Things people might feel and associate with the colour pink are: love, romance, pigs, sex, pink roses, etc.

Blue

Blue is a very powerful colour. It can make people stay at your website longer because it relaxes them and calms them down. Just think about running water or blue skies.

People associate darker blues with authority, like businesspeople in blue suits or police officers. People will buy more quickly from authoritative figures or businesses. Wear a blue suit if you publish your picture on your website.

Things people might feel and associate with the colour blue are: water, rain, sky, police officers, business suits, ocean, cool, etc.

Orange

Orange can create a feeling of warmth and comfort. Just think about the sun or going from cold to hot – a very attractive prospect as I look out of my window at the frost all over my car! Orange can make your prospects feel more comfortable ordering from you.

Things people might feel and associate with the colour orange are: sunshine, oranges, sunsets, warmth, fire, candlelight, etc.

Green

Green makes people feel secure. Use it in your privacy policy, guarantee or on your secure ordering page. Money is green; when people have more of it they feel more financially secure.

Things people might feel and associate with the colour green are: grass, trees, luck, spring, life, money, etc.

Purple

Purple is associated with royalty and wealth. Look at the old films of medieval kings and queens wearing purple. People have been conditioned to respect royalty all their lives. This association could help your customers respect your business.

Things people might feel and associate with the colour purple are: grapes, richness, wisdom, royalty, etc.

White

Use a white background on your website. People associate white with trust and honesty. Both of these qualities will help you sell more products.

Things people might feel and associate with the colour white are: purity, surrender, peace, doves, milk, innocence, honesty, etc.

Black

Use black text on a white background because people associate the colour combination with professionalism and sophistication.

Things people might feel and associate with the colour black are: night, style, evil, depth, cats, sophistication, elegance, etc.

Brown

Use brown coloured text for your business name because it relates to credibility. It will help your customers trust your business quicker. Brown is also a colour of richness and warmth.

Things people might feel and associate with the colour brown are: earth, stability, wood, leather, chocolate, etc.

Gold/silver

Gold and silver are considered valuable. Use those colours on your product's packaging to make it look more valuable. They're also considered rare metals. People like to buy and own things that are considered rare. Use the colours silver and gold in your ad copy with a limited time offer.

Things people might feel and associate with the colours gold and silver are: jewellery, wealth, rare items, etc.

Numbers and symbols

Lucky numbers: Some people think the number seven is lucky. Other people think the number eight is luckier. These numbers would be persuasive in a gambling advert or for anything relating to money and prosperity.

The number one: Some people consider the number one as being the best, and as first place. The number one might work well for business or athletic copy.

Hearts: Some people associate a heart shape with love and romance. A heart would influence people to buy if you were selling roses.

Trees and plants: Some people associate plants and trees with life. These symbols should compel people to buy health or medical products.

Red traffic lights: Some people associate a red traffic light with stopping. This could grab a person's attention so that they focus on your advert.

Money: Some people associate money with greed or being rich. Money objects would sell business and stock opportunities well.

Light bulbs: Some people associate these with great ideas and brainwaves, which could work well for promoting new inventions or life-changing products.

Water: Some people consider water to convey messages of freshness or cleanliness, and also with power, especially moving water such as a waterfall.

Ribbons: Some people may associate ribbons with seduction, luxury or sexuality.

Traditional Eastern symbols (such as statues of Buddha): Some people associate these symbols with peace and relaxation.

Tips for presenting information

The following list offers 24 ideas to help you find the perfect way to present information to your audience:

1   Most people want to feel or be intelligent. Tell them in your copy how smart they would be if they invested in your product.

2   Most people in life end up replacing items that are out of date, used-up, broken or old. Give your current customers repeat-buyer discounts.

3 Most people want a clean environment. Tell your prospects that you'll donate a percentage of your profits to help clean up the environment.

4 Most people want to eat good food. Give your customers free coupons to a nice restaurant when they purchase your product.

5 Most people need or want new information to absorb. Give your customers a free tip sheet when they purchase your product.

6 Most people want to avoid or end pain. Tell your prospects how much pain and how many problems they will avoid or end if they buy your product.

7 Most people want to gain pleasure. Tell your prospects how much pleasure or the benefits they will gain if they purchase your product.

8 Most people want to win over others. Tell your prospects how their family or friends will admire them if they buy your product.

9 Most people want to have good health and live longer. Give your prospects free coupons to a fitness club when they buy your product.

10 Most people want to belong to something or to a select group. Give your prospects free membership into your club when they buy your product.

11 Most people are curious about things that could affect their life. Use words and phrase like 'Secret', 'Top Secret' or 'Confidential' in your ad.

12 Most people want to make extra money or be their own boss. Give your prospects the option to join your free re-seller programme when they buy.

13 Most people want to save time and spend their extra time enjoying life. Offer your prospects fast shipping, fast ordering options, etc.

14 Most people want life to be easier. Give your prospects easy ordering instructions, easy product instructions, etc.

15 Most people want to feel secure and safe. Tell your prospects that you have secure ordering and a privacy policy.

16 Most people want to receive compliments for their achievements. Give your prospects plenty of compliments for buying your product.

Selling for Entrepreneurs

17 Most people like surprises because it's a change of pace from the regular routine. Tell your prospects that they will get a surprise free bonus for ordering.

18 Most people want to invest in their future. Tell your prospects to 'invest in our product' instead of 'buy our product'.

19 Most people want the latest and newest things in life. Use words and phrases in your copy like 'New', 'Just Released', etc.

20 Most people want to solve their problems. Tell your prospects what problems they have and how your product can solve them.

21 Most people want to make the people around them happy. Tell your prospects how happy their friends or family will be if they buy your product.

22 Most people want to get over their obstacles so they can achieve their goals. Tell your prospects what goals they'll achieve by ordering your product.

23 Most people don't want to miss out on a major opportunity that they could regret in the future. Tell your prospects you'll be raising the price shortly.

24 Most people want to associate with others who have the same interests. Give your prospects free membership in a private chatroom just for them.

Web bonus

At our website, **www.forentrepreneursbooks.com**, click on the 'Selling for Entrepreneurs' button. On the link for Chapter Eleven you will find dozens more powerful sales phrases.

Key points

→ Influencing is a powerful skill and a serious responsibility.

→ Influential people are exciting to be around.

→ Influential people are not pushy, bullying or manipulative. They don't need to be anything underhand or insincere, and neither do you.

→ The way you feel about selling will have a real impact on your capacity to influence.

→ Robert Cialdini identified rules about influence that you can use to your advantage.

→ 'Hypnotic' sales flow naturally, causing the prospect to feel the emotions, experiences and benefits you want them to feel.

→ In addition to words, colours and images can be hugely effective in influencing.

Next steps

What action will you take to apply the information in this chapter? By when will you do it?

_____

_____

_____

_____

The sales process

Chapter Twelve

Research has shown that 92 per cent of companies stop following up after four knock-backs, but that over 60 per cent of customers say no at least five times when making unusual or perceived high-risk purchases. So 8 per cent of businesses are getting more than 60 per cent of the sales! Are you one of them? Wouldn't you like to be?

'No' now can sometimes be 'yes' later. Or it may be 'no' for ever. The trick is to figure out which camp a certain 'no' falls into and then respond appropriately.

Do you have enough stages in your sales process?

Constantly chasing prospects after they've shown an interest can be soul-destroying and border on pushy salesmanship. But by having a longer sales process, prospects are moved from one stage to the next over a period of time, are constantly informed and educated, and are reminded of your services. Just because they didn't buy today doesn't mean they're not interested in what you sell at all, so ensure you have at least seven stages in your sales process, including emails, mail-shots, brochures, PR, web downloads and phone calls.

By selling the value of your offering through various different sales techniques, you can start to build rapport and establish confidence. Customers often don't know what questions to ask, so the more information you can provide, the better.

 If you work just for money, you'll never make it. But if you love what you are doing, and always put the customer first, success will be yours.

RAY KROK

Why create barriers?

We've all come across companies that have utterly illogical sales processes, and even when we want to buy from them, they make the process painful and difficult. My favourite recent example was a company offering an internet access account that you could only buy through their website (you want me to buy it online when I have no online access to begin with?).

Last year, I attempted to buy some early Christmas presents after being inspired by a beautiful window display. However, it didn't take long for me to realise that the layout of the store was not designed to be customer friendly. After looking around hopelessly for a while, attempting to ask members of staff who ignored me, and even taking one item to the abandoned till point, I gave up and left empty-handed.

Mrs Grundy herself constituted a barrier to buying.

I often encourage my clients to explore customer service in action by visiting a store or calling a hotline for a product or service they know almost nothing about. The best service will inform, educate and direct, even if it doesn't create a direct buying need. The worst will leave people confused and frustrated. I won't name names, but I'm sure you can think of some high street examples that achieve this unwanted goal on a regular basis.

The more barriers these companies put between themselves and their customer, the worse business gets. Throw too many ifs and buts into the process and you can kiss the customer goodbye, probably for ever.

Take a good hard look at the processes you've built into your sales funnel that could be preventing enthusiastic customers from doing business with you. It could be a slightly uncomfortable exercise, but better that than an empty bank account.

Making it easy

The first rule for any business has to be, 'Make it easy for the customer to buy from you'. In order to purchase your product or service, your customer should not have to navigate any obstacles. You should make every effort to make the purchase process as easy and painless as possible. Remove any barriers that might prevent customers from purchasing, or give them an opportunity to change their mind about purchasing.

Unfortunately, at every stage of the sale, you have the potential of losing the customer. Undoubtedly, some of you reading this paragraph will be operating in industry sectors that must comply with endless legal, financial or regulatory guidance. You may believe that this doesn't apply to you. But I implore you to look again at your sales process.

Don't require the customer to complete complicated forms or provide lots of unnecessary information during the order process. Your application, membership information-request and order forms should request only the information that relates directly to the purchase. You can always ask for additional information as the relationship builds.

How to purchase your product should be blatantly obvious to all potential customers. The number they should ring, address they should write to or site they should visit must be crystal clear.

Offer a variety of payment options. Preferred payment options vary across regions. Do not alienate potential purchasers by not offering any payment options that they are accustomed to and familiar with.

Once you've got a prospect ready to take action, keep the order process as simple as possible. Do not give the customer any distractions from the primary objective of closing the sale. Removing any roadblocks from the order process will help instil confidence in purchasers and increase the number of completed orders.

Your entire sales process should be relevant to the scale of the purchase. Are your products and services expensive, unusual or complex? Even if your business is focused on staple items at average market prices, it's always worth putting yourself back into the mindset of someone who's never experienced it before. If you sell food, where is it sourced from, how is it prepared? Or perhaps clothing? What body shape does this item flatter, how is it best to wear it?

What if you don't want their business?

But what if you've decided that this prospect is actually not right for you? As an entrepreneur with integrity, it could be that you don't want their business. Here are three reasons why a prospect might not be right for your business.

The work compromises your values

You're offered a contract or a relationship that helps promote third world slave labour, pollutes the environment or exploits workers without due compensation. Perhaps you belong to a faith group and the work could violate your beliefs. You have every right to turn down work that bothers your spiritual or social conscience. You will sleep better at night and possess a clear mind to better focus on your work.

The work compromises your life balance

Sometimes, too much work is a good sign that your business is growing by leaps and bounds. But what if you run the hazard of taking on too much? Something will give, in the quality of either your work or your service to existing customers.

The work compromises your professional worth

Never dedicate your valuable time to be compensated at slave wages or way below your margin. Your rate reflects your worth, and if you value your highly skilled work you will charge accordingly. By low-balling your billing, you only undervalue yourself. It could be better to lose the client and take that time to serve another customer who respects your value as a professional.

The customer's satisfaction is paramount to any competitive business. But it's your business and you must reserve the right to protect your worth and integrity. By politely refusing the occasional instance where a customer keeps you from maintaining your high standards or living a balanced lifestyle, you leave room for success that's more than just monetary.

Avoiding pushiness

How can you build a sales process that doesn't feel like pushy salesmanship?

Create an irresistible offer

You have to give McDonald's credit for the 'supersize me' offer. It may only generate another 40 or 50 pence per sale, but because it's such an irresistible offer, more than 30 per cent of customers will say yes. And that 40 or 50 pence is almost all profit, as the company's fixed costs have already been absorbed in the price of the main item. The scale of the offer must be relative to the purchase, but once you have acquired the customer you can start to create lifetime value.

Add point of sale purchases

Those associated purchases or impulse buys that the supermarkets put by the checkouts aren't an accident. Small low-price items that are perfectly positioned will face the least resistance from a buyer who's already decided to make a purchase from you.

Get prospects hooked with a free sample

Prospects that test your product or service risk-free will hopefully recognise its value and continue purchasing what you offer. Or even better, your prospect will get 'hooked' on your product or service and won't be able to live without it. And the fact that it was given away free will compel them to return the favour by continuing to purchase from you. This principle is called the 'law of reciprocity'. Simply stated, people naturally feel an obligation to return favours as a way of expressing their thanks (see also page 172).

Educate customers to use a product differently

This might mean showing prospects how to benefit more from using associated products in conjunction; buy this much, get this one free and so on. Remember the famous story of the shampoo company that doubled its sales with the simple phrase 'rinse and repeat'.

'Other customers who bought XYZ also bought…'

This clever approach is used by many online retailers to position more of their product lines in front of customers who might be interested. Where key components like batteries aren't included, make sure you offer them.

Communicate with customers more often

Communicate with customers more often about your full offering as part of your sales process. This could take the form of newsletters, emails, mailshots, letters, advertising and PR, events, brochures and literature.

Consider what else your customers buy that you could sell

The more you know about your customers, the more back-end products and services you can provide. This means that their main purchase simply becomes a foot-in-the-door, and now you can increase the frequency of purchase and average spend.

Offer incentives and discounts

By understanding the lifetime value of customers – that is, the total value of their spend during their time as a customer – you can decide how much you are prepared to discount to get them back through the door.

Position yourself as an expert

Position yourself as an expert to gain the trust and confidence of prospects. Through your PR, direct communications and website, you can provide information, reviews, reports and details on your specialist area. Customers often don't know the right questions to ask, so help them out.

Review your ordering process

See whether you are making it difficult for people to buy from you. Look at your website cart abandonment rate or try a mystery shopper service.

Are you focusing on the benefits?

Customers only care about what you can do for them. Benefits build rapport by demonstrating that you understand their point of view. If you don't know what they are, ask your customers. You can never know too much about why people buy from you.

Are you and your staff selling?

By testing, measuring and analysing all your marketing and sales processes, you can see where the majority of initial sales and back-end sales take place. Are your best people in place to exploit those opportunities? Do you have the ten characteristics of a powerful sales personality? If not, these are the ones to develop:

→ a high level of self-confidence and self-esteem;

→ accepting full responsibility for results;

→ above average ambitions;

→ high levels of empathy for prospects, customers and colleagues;

→ goal-oriented;

→ above average willpower;

→ determined and hard working;

→ belief in self, company and products;

→ absolute honesty;

→ strong verbal and non-verbal skills to turn strangers into friends.

Build a strong relationship

Having great customer relationships is a privilege. Without them, your company would have no revenue. Yet human nature being what it is, we tend to focus on the tasks we have to complete and see customers as being a distraction or even a nuisance because they take our time and our energy.

Even people who have nothing to do but look after customers can fall into the trap of seeing a customer with a special need or difficult problem as someone who is stopping them from serving other customers. And customers with a complaint are seen by most of us as a threat, someone to be got rid of quickly.

You should build an organisation that works for your customers, not one that makes your customers work for your organisation. You should do things quickly and make it easy for your customers to do business with you. You want to create policies and processes that ensure your customers are looked after.

People want to do business with companies they like. Does your company have a likeable personality in the eyes of your customers? How do they want you to look? Does your image match that? What do they want you to support? Does your sponsorship or investment pro-gramme reflect that? How do they want you to act? Is your behaviour consistent with that?

Key points

→ The sales process rarely has a neat beginning, middle and end. The process can be a constant circle, and everything you can do to simplify your involvement will make selling easier and less stressful.

→ Of course, there are legal, financial or regulatory guidelines that rightly exist to protect all parties. But making it hard to buy from you will mean only the really determined prospect battles through to the end.

→ If you have barriers in the sales process, ensure that they are there to help you identify prospects that aren't right for you, as opposed to simply an assault course for genuine customers.

→ Stepping back from your sales process will help you see opportunities to introduce sales techniques that keep suspects, prospects and customers close at hand without additional work for you.

→ Entrepreneurial salespeople create businesses that customers want to buy from.

Next steps

What action will you take to apply the information in this chapter? By
when will you do it?

_____

_____

_____

_____

Index

self-knowledge 34
Selfridges 52
sensory persuasion 180
seven (number) 10
shopping cart abandonment rate
141, 198
'signpost, say and summarise' 81
'six degrees of separation' 82, 84
social proof 14
law of 173
and purchase decision 13
Socrates 106
Southon, Mike 130
staff 51
statisfy.com 142
stories, power of 178–9
strapline 78
successful entrepreneurs
characteristics of 111, 114–17
symbols 186–7

task-focused buyers 9
telephone prospecting 65, 66, 67
telephone sales 62, 67
testimonials 93
use of in copywriting 139
testing 43
and direct mail 147
30-second commercial 77
time management 25–6
time-wasters 25, 61
tone, and cold calling 69–70
tree and plant symbols 187
trial close questions
and closing a sale 127–8
and pitching 80
Trout, Jack 149

USP (unique selling point) 40, 45–7,
79, 145
defining your 49–51
identifying your 45–6

value, understanding of 44

water symbol 187
websites 135–6, 139–42
and autoresponders 141–2
capturing visitor details 140–1
content of 140
links to 136
mistakes 142–3
and newsletters 141
ordering process 141
and pay-per-click advertising 134–5
ranking of 135–6
shopping cart abandonment rate
141, 198
tracking path of visitors to 142
use of colours 184–6
writing good sales copy 136–9
'what' questions 160–1
white (colour) 186
winning edge concept 24, 108
Wolff, Jurgen
Focus: The Power of Targeted
Thinking 33
Wright, Steve 62
writing game 138

Xerox 41

yellow (colour) 184

Ziglar, Zig 106